Srimad Bhagavad Gita - A Summary Study

OrangeBooks Publication

1st Floor, Rajhans Arcade, Mall Road, Kohka, Bhilai, Chhattisgarh 490020

Website: **www.orangebooks.in**

© **Copyright, 2025, Author**

All rights reserved. No part of this book may be reproduced, stored in a retrieval system, or transmitted, in any form by any means, electronic, mechanical, magnetic, optical, chemical, manual, photocopying, recording or otherwise, without the prior written consent of its writer.

First Edition, 2025

ISBN: 978-93-6554-679-8

SRIMAD BHAGAVAD GITA
A SUMMARY STUDY

Based on the teachings from Bhagavad Gita as it is by his divine grace A.C Bhaktivedanta Swami Srila Prabhupada

GRISHA LAVINGIA

OrangeBooks Publication
www.orangebooks.in

Introduction

SRIMAD BHAGAVAD GITA, also considered as the manual of life. A book which contains answers to all questions, be it material or spiritual.

In our material life, we are constantly struggling for something or the other. Even if we achieve something, we are not satisfied and endeavor for something greater. In this way, we pass many births and many deaths and are still struck in this unlimited cycle and don't understand the ultimate goal of life.

The Gita or the Gitopanishad was a conversation which took place between the supreme personality of Godhead Sri Krishna and his intimate friend and devotee Arjuna.

We are all living entities and are conditioned by the material nature. In the Gita, Lord Krishna addresses conditioned souls like us to understand what this precious human form of life is made for and how are we wasting it by engaging in all sorts of silly things that are absolutely useless.

We think of ourselves as this to temporary body and engage in material activities without knowing our actual constitutional position as eternal souls serving Krishna.

SRIMAD BHAGAVAD GITA preaches Krishna consciousness and is considered a guide to devotional service spoken by the Supreme personality of Godhead Krishna himself.

Krishna is the Supreme enjoyer and we as souls are in this material world to serve the Supreme Lord and finally go back to godhead.

This pure conversation between The Supreme Personality of Godhead and Arjuna teach us **how to serve Krishna.**

One who reads **SRIMAD BHAGAVAD GITA** with sincerity and devotion towards Krishna would never fall and will continue to fulfill the mission of human form of life. He/She is considered to be a divine soul.

This is my small effort towards preaching Krishna Consciousness in this world.

I am not a perfect writer, but I have tried my best to interpret the correct meaning of each chapter.

So here I present, to all the readers." A Summary Study of **SRIMAD BHAGAVAD GITA"**.

This book is inspired by:

SHRIMAD BHAGAVAD GITA As it is by His Divine Grace (HDC) A.C Bhakti Vedanta Swami Srila Prabhupad, the founder Acharya of International Society for Krishna Consciousness (ISKON).

There are many commenters or books on Bhagavad Gita in which the authors try to mend the knowledge given by Krishna in their own way and present a contaminated version of the divine Gitopnishad. But the knowledge given in Bhagavad Gita As It Is is passed down through disciplic succession coming directly from the Supreme Personality of Godhead Lord.

Srila Prabhupad started ISKON community and has preached Krishna consciousness all over the world and therefore inspired by his book, this is a summary study of the Gita.

Index

Chapter One
"Observing The Armies In The Battlefield Of Kurukshetra" 1

Chapter Two
Contents of Gita Summarized 7

Chapter Three
"Karma Yoga" 18

Chapter Four
"Transcendental knowledge" 23

Chapter Five
"Karma-yoga. - Action in Krishna Consciousness" 28

Chapter Six
Dhyana Yoga 32

Chapter Seven
"Knowledge of the Absolute" 38

Chapter Eight
"Attaining the Supreme" 42

Chapter Nine
"The Most Confidential Knowledge" 46

Chapter Ten
The Opulence of the Absolute 51

Chapter Eleven
The Universal Form 56

Chapter Twelve
    Devotional Service 64

Chapter Thirteen
    Nature, the Enjoyer and Consciousness. 68

Chapter Fourteen
    The Three Modes of Material Nature... 73

Chapter Fifteen
    The Yoga of the Supreme Person 77

Chapter Sixteen
    The Divine and Demonic Natures. 81

Chapter Seventeen
    The divisions of Faith. 85

Chapter Eighteen
    Conclusion – The Perfection of Renunciation............................... 89

    Conclusion 101

Chapter One
"Observing The Armies In The Battlefield Of Kurukshetra"

The first chapter of **Bhagavad Gita** is basically **setting of the scene**. **How** and **why** Lord Krishna had to **speak** the **Bhagavad Gita**? Why was Arjuna thrown into illusion and had a **lot of doubts** about whether he should **fight the war or not?**

Dhritarashtra said, "O Sanjaya, after my sons and the sons of Pandu assembled at pilgrimage of Kurukshetra desiring to fight what did they do?"

Sanjay had divine vision and was telling everything that was happening in the battlefield to Dhritarashtra.

This very first verse of Bhagavad Gita is spoken by Dhritarashtra as he was scared that his sons might lose because he knew that why they were on the wrong side. The Pandavas were on the right path as Lord Krishna was himself was present with them. And wherever there is Krishna, there is victory.

Sanjaya said "O King, after looking at the military formation by the Pandavas, Duryodhana went to his teacher and spoke the following words."

Duryodhana said to his teacher that, the great army of the Pandavas was arranged in a very excellent manner. He was basically trying to tell the defects of his teacher because somewhere even Duryodhana knew that he was going to lose as Krishna was not on their side.

Arjuna and Bhima were the most excellent fighters and warriors on the Pandavas side. But, there were many equivalent fighter such as Yuyudrana, Virata and Drupada.

There were great heroic fighters such as Dhristketu, Cekitana, Kashiraja, Purojit, Kumbjoj and Saibya.

There were also the sons of Draupadi and the son of Subhadra "Abhimanyu".

And Yudhamanyu all these were great fighters.

Duryodhana further said " But for your information, O' best of Brahamanas, listen that there are many great warriors who are especially trained and qualified to lead my military force, there are great personalities like you, Bhisma, Karna, Krpa, Aswattama, Vikrama and son of Somadatta called Bhuri……

Basically, Duryodhana is trying to satisfy himself by saying all these as he has the fear that he might lose.

He thinks that are great fighters on his side who are expert with many weapons and military signs and can give their lives for his sake. He further says: "Our strength is unlimited as we are protected by our grandfather Bhishma, whereas the Pandavas are protected by Bhima and therefore their strength is limited".

Duryodhana is expressing his ego by saying this "In this Kalyuga, we are also the same like Duryodhana.

He further instructed all the fighters of his to give full respect and support to grandfather Bhishma as without Bhishma there was no scope of winning for Duryodhana.

After then, Bhishma blew his conch shell very loudly which made a sound like the roar of a lion giving Duryodhana joy.

Even grandfather Bhishma knew that he cannot win as Lord Krishna was not on their side. He was just fighting as a matter of duty.

Every war is terrible. And the war of Mahabharata was the most terrible of all wars. So, at the beginning conch shells, drums, bugles, trumpets and horns were all suddenly sounded.

On the other side, Lord Krishna and Arjuna were both on an excellent Chariot which was drawn by white horses. Both of them blew their conch shells.

Lord Krishna blew conch shells named Panchjanya, Arjuna blew his, called Devadatta and Bhima blew his very terrific conch shell named Paundra.

Along with them, King Yudhisthira also blew Conch shell named Ananta Vijaya Nakula and Sahadeva blew theirs named Sughesi and Manipuspaka respectively.

Even the king of Kashi, Sikhandi, Dhristadyuna, Virata, Satyaki, Drupada, the sons of Draupadi and all the others blew their respective conch shells.

The sound of all of these conch shells vibrated so loud in the sky that it shattered the hearts of all the Sons of Dhritarashtra.

At that time, Arjuna who was seated on the chariot which beared the flag marked with Hanuman took up his bow gardiva and prepared to fight. After looking at the Kauravas he spoke to Lord Krishna as follows:

He said "O Lord, Please draw this Chariot in the middle of the battlefield so that I can see all those present, who are prepared to fight".

So this is the beginning of Arjuna's confusion.

Lord Krishna by his great mercy was the chariot - driver of Arjuna. Krishna is very compassionate towards his devotees and can do anything for the benefit of them.

Arjuna wanted to see all the fighters who had come to battle field to just please the evil-minded Duryodhana.

The war of Mahabharata took place due to the stubbornness of Duryodhana.

Sanjaya further said: "having been addressed by Arjuna like this, Lord Krishna drew the chariot in the middle of battlefield. And after reaching there, in presence of

Bhishma, Drona and many fighters from the world, he asked Arjuna to see all the kurus assembled there. "

Arjuna, standing there, in the middle of both the armies, could see all his family members and relatives, his fathers, grandfathers, teachers, maternal uncles, sons, grandsons, and many friends and well-wishers.

Aften seeing all of them, he became overwhelmed and spoke the following words...

Arjuna said: " O my Dear Krishna seeing all my friends and relatives here, I feel all my limbs shaking and my mouth drying. My body is trembling. My hairs are standing one end and my bow Gandiva is slipping from my hand. My skin is burning.

"O killer of Kesi demon, I can only see this war as a cause of a misfortune and cannot stand here any longer. I am forgetting myself."

"O Dear Krishna, I can see no good by killing my own family members. I do not want any such victory, kingdom or happiness."

Arjuna is driven by his illusion and the attachment for his family members.

We often come across such situations where we are driven by such illusions and cannot differentiate between the right and wrong, just like Arjuna.

Arjuna furthered said: "O Krishna, what benefit will such kingdom, happiness or even life given when, for whom we desire all this are standing against us in the battlefield."

"O Madhusudhana, when all my teachers, fathers, sons, grandfathers, fathers- in-law, grandsons and other relative are ready to give up their lives for me, then why should I kill them?"

"O Maintainer of all living entities, I ain't ready to fight those even if I get all the three worlds in exchange. What pleasure will we get after killing the sons of Dhritarashtra?"

Arjuna is so much attached to his family members that he is forgetting his duty and that all his family members did wrong at some point in their lives.

Sometimes to get benefit of our own, we must leave something which is very precious to us.

Arjuna continued saying: " What will we gain after killing our own family members. Sin will overcome us, if we do such things. O' Krishna, you are the husband of Goddess of Fortune, (Lakshmi). I think that it is not proper to kill the Sons of Dhritarashtra."

Arjuna is forgetting his duty of fighting and is afraid that he might commit a sin.

He continued saying: "O Govinda, even if the hearts of the sons of Dhritarashtra are over taken by greed end they are ready to kill each other's family members, but why we should we do these kind of acts knowing that it is a crime."

Arjuna is afraid that is figuring a war, his whole family would be destroyed. And if it happens, rest of the family would be engaged in irreligion resulting in destroying the family tradition.

And when a family engages itself in irreligion, women of a family are polluted resulting in unwanted population.

Arjuna further said: " Women make up the family, and if unwanted population occurs it would destroy all the rituals of the family. And the ancestors of such families would eventually fall down.

And such a family's traditions are destroyed. And those whose family's traditions are destroyed are always dwelling in hell."

Arjuna continued saying: "And how strange it is that we are ready to do such great sins. We are killing our known family just for the sake of royal happiness.

O' Janardana, it is better that the sons of Dhritarashtra only kill me when I am unarmed on the battlefield. "

Sanjaya who was giving the description of the events taking place on the battlefield of Kurukshetra to Dhritarashtra said:

"And having spoken these words, Arjuna, overwhelmed by grief kept aside his bow, Gandiva and sat on the chariot."

This was the first chapter of Bhagavad Gita where in we got to know the setiing of the scene and like Arjuna, even we must be having similar doubts as we are always driven by our illusion.

Chapter Two
Contents of Gita Summarized

We read about the queries and the doubts of Arjuna in the previous chapter. Now from the second chapter Lord Krishna will give the knowledge of Gita. In this chapter he will mainly explain about the difference between the body and the soul. This chapter will also be a summary of the upcoming content in the next chapters.

Sanjaya said: "O King, after seeing Arjuna's eyes full of tears and seeing him sad and depressed, Lord Krishna spoke the following words"

Lord Krishna is very compassionate towards his devotees and Arjuna was his very intimate devotee. Seeing him in such a state he decided to solve Arjuna's doubts and recited the entire Bhagavad Gita to clear Arjuna's confusion.

Lord Krishna said: "My dear Arjuna, how have these kind of attachments and impurities attacked you. They don't suit a warrior like you nor do they lead to higher Planets. They only lead to infamy."

Lord Krishna was reminding Arjuna of his duty of fighting as he was much driven by his attachment.

He further said: "O Arjuna, do not lead to such attachments and impurities. They do not suit you. Attachment is merely a weakness. Give up such weakness of heart and fight."

Many times we forget our duties due to our own attachments. But these attachments lead to nothing. They are just a weakness. We should give them up and fulfill our duty without expecting anything from it.

Arjuna said: "O Krishna, how can I attack Bhishma and Drona with my arrows when they can be worshiped by me.

"It is better to live by begging than kill our own relatives and live at the cost of the lives of such great souls. If they will be killed everything that we will enjoy will be tainted with blood."

He further said: "O killer of enemies, we do not even know which is better to fight or not. If we kill the Sons of Dhritarashtra, we will not be able to live.

"O Lord, I don't know what to do now? What is my duty? I surrender unto you, now please guide me about what is best for me?"

This is the sign of a true devotee, when he fully surrenders unto the Supreme Lord Krishna. Krishna ensures that he will clear all his doubts and guide him on the right way.

Arjuna further said. "O my Lord, even if, I get unlimited pleasures and prosperities, I cant find any way to derive my grief."

Sanjaya said: " Arjuna, in extreme grief said to Krishna that he shall not fight, and then went silent."

Dhritarashtra was very happy after hearing this statement of Sanjaya as he was afraid' that the Pandavas will kill his sons, because he was so much attached to them. When you are so much attached to something, we always have the fear that we might lose that thing.

Now, in the middle of both the enemies, Krishna, the supreme Personality of Godhead, smiling and standing before a grief-stricken Arjuna spoke the following words.

Krishna was smiling as he was going to speak something which no one in the three worlds knew till now.

The Supreme Personality of Godhead said: "O Arjuna, you are speaking very wise words, but at the same time you are speaking it for them who don't deserve them. Those are who are wise neither mourn for the living nor for the dead."

"Moreover there was never a time when I did not exist, you all these fighters and kings did not exist. Nor in future there will be a time like this."

Why is our body moving? Why are our hands and legs working? Why are all the organ systems in body working properly? There must be something inside our body which makes it work.

The answer is consciousness. This Consciousness is for there because of the presence of the soul.

This soul is continuously passing, from childhood to adulthood and from adulthood to old age. At the time of death, this soul passes to another body. The consciousness from the previous body goes to another and hence, the body stops working

A wise person knows this nature of the soul and is not deluded by such change.

Krishna further tells that this coming and going of happiness and distress is like changing seasons.

Basically this is the dual nature of life in this material world. Anything there is not permanent. There can't be happiness forever nor can there be distress, with happiness comes distress. Likewise with respect comes insult and with victory comes defeat. We need to understand this duality and tolerate it just as we tolerate seasons.

Krishna said: "The person who is steady and not disturbed by happiness and distress, is eligible for liberation"

Some saintly persons have studied the nature of the body and the Soul and have concluded that for the body there is no endurance and for the soul there is no change.

The soul is spread all over the body. But we should know that the body is destructible while the soul is imperishable.

Krishna Said:" As the material Body of the living entity (soul) is destructible, it is sure to come to an end. Therefore fight Arjuna!"

Now Krishna is trying to tell that all the relatives of Arjuna are residing in their body and therefore even if he doesn't fight their bodies are sure to come to an end. So Arjuna should give up his attachments, understand the difference between a living entity (soul) and his body, and perform his duty.

The one who thinks that it is the soul which kills, or the one who thinks that the soul is already dead. Neither of them are in knowledge.

The soul neither has a birth nor has a death. It just exists and that is the truth.

It has never come into being and never will come into being. It is unborn, ever- existing, eternal, indestructible and immeasurable. The body can be dead but the soul can never be.

Krishna further said: "How can a person kill anyone one or cause any one kill after knowing that the soul is eternal, indestructible and unborn."

We get the fruits of our actions. But to execute them, the soul needs a particular aid. And that is the body. A type of body is needed to execute some fruits and after those fruits are executed, the soul changes the body and that causes the deter of the body.

Just as we use the old clothes, throw them and wear new ones. Similarly the soul accepts a body and when the body is useless, it changes the body into new ones. And this cycle of birth and death continues.

A Soul can neither be cut into pieces by any weapon, nor burned by fire, nor moister by water, nor withered by wind.

A body has an age but soul doesn't, it is unmovable, unbreakable, everlasting it cannot be changed and is present- everywhere. Its eternal nature is same.

After knowing that soul is invisible, cannot be conceived and cannot be understood by our mundane material senses, one should not have a greed for the body. He should just engage himself in knowing about the Soul.

Krishna further said: " Even if you think that the soul is destined to be born and die, then also, there is no reason to be in distress."

Though, the soul is indestructible but even if one thinks that it always takes birth and dies, there is no reason to be depressed as it is destined.

Birth and death are two sides of the same coin. One who has taken birth is sure to die and one who has died will take birth again.

We sometimes cry for things which are destined to happen and the same was with Arjuna.

Krishna said: "In the beginning of the creation, the living beings are unmanifested. When the creation is going on, this living beings manifest. At the time of destruction, they are unmanifested. Then what is the reason for lament."

This creation and destruction of universe will further be told in the eight chapter.

Now some people think of the Soul as amazing and some describe it amazing. And some hear it amazing. But others cannot understand the Soul even after hearing about it.

Even after hearing about the knowledge we return in illusion. But one should try to execute it. Knowing this knowledge, one should not grieve for any living being.

Arjuna was a Kshtriya. It is the duty of kshtriya to fight. And Arjuna's fight was for Religious Principles. The war of Mahabharata was fought to establish righteousness or religion. Therefore, there was no need for hesitation in accomplishing his duty of fighting.

Krishna said: "O Arjuna, The kshtriya for whom such opportunities of fighting for religious principles come, are happy as they can get a transfer on higher Planets."

"But if, however if you do not fight, you will incur sin of neglecting your duties which will hamper your reputation as a fighter. And for kshatriya, disrespect is greater than death."

"The great men, who always speak about your honor and glories will think that you left the battlefield out of fear. And they will think of you of no importance. "

Krishna is again reminding Arjuna that he should not hesitate from his duties even if he had to fight with his closed ones for righteousness.

He further said: "Listen, O son of Kunti", your enemies will say you many unkind words and doubt upon your ability. What could be more painful to you?"

"O Arjuna, either you will be killed on this battlefield and will attain heavenly planet or you will kill the son of Dhritarashtra and will get the kingdom on this earth. Does not matter, just fight because you are fighting to establish religion."

One should not think about happiness and distress, victory or defeat, loss or gain while completing his duties. He should just do it for Krishna. If one does his work for the happiness of Krishna, he will not incur any kind of sin.

We should do all our work for Krishna because he is the supreme Lord and Supreme enjoyer.

In terms of Karma, one who works with such attitude of serving Krishna will free himself from the bondage of this material world.

Arjuna wasn't fighting because of his fear. But even the desire to serve Krishna can free us from this type of fear.

Now here, Arjuna was in State of indession. In such state, one is surrounded by many thoughts and is confused. Therefore, one should be firm upon his decision and only and such a person can progress.

In this world, we think ourselves as the enjoyer, such person are said to men of small knowledge by Krishna. They are very much attracted their own sense gratification. Their only aim is to enjoy their senses and they don't think beyond it. They want elevation to higher planets to enjoy but don't want to perform devotional service to the Supreme Personality of Godhead.

Such people, who are very much attracted to material opulence and sense gratification cannot fix their minds in performing devotional Service.

There are three modes of material nature- goodness, passion & ignorance.

The Vedas mainly deal with these three modes. But these modes bind us from these world. Therefore, one should transcend them. One should become free from all the dualities of life and be established in the Self.

A small well can serve some purposes of a man. But a greater reservoir of water can serve all the purposes of a small well.

Just like that a man who knows the real aim of Vedas can serve all the purposes of the Vedas.

Now, all the Vedas reach to one Conclusion that is: Krishna is the Supreme Lord and we as Souls are eternal servants of Krishna and that is our constitutional position. Therefore, we should engage in the devotional service of Krishna. That is the real aim of the Vedas. Devotional service is the real essence of Vedas.

Krishna further said: " You just have the right to perform your duties, but you never the right to the fruits of your actions. Never consider yourself as the cause of the results of the actions. But, never be attached to not doing your duty."

This is one of the most popular verse of the Bhagavad Gita.: The results of our actions are not in our hands. You can just perform your duty. But that does not mean you can stop doing your duty. You have to do without expecting the fruits of it.

One should be equal in all situations. One should perform his duty without thinking of success or failure. And such a state is called yoga.

Krishna says that one should stay away from all those actions which are restricted in devotional service. And in such a state one should surrender unto the Lord. Those who want to enjoy the fruits of their actions always remain in distress.

A man who is in devotional service gets rid from the good and bad reactions of life. And does not have to take birth again. Therefore, one should strive for yoga which is out of all work.

And such a man engaged in devotional service. Goes back to Godhead. Great Sages have freed themselves from the results of their actions by engaging in devotional service.

Then material world is like a dense forest of illusion. When one's intelligence goes beyond this dense forest by devotional service, he achieves transcendence.

When one is no longer attracted to material enjoyments and is situated in self-realization (thinking of one's self as eternal Servants of Krishna) he achieves divine consciousness.

Arjuna asked:" O My Lord, How Can we recognize a person situated in transcendence? How does he sit? How does he speak and what is his language?"

The Supreme Personality of Godhead replied: "When a man gives up his sense of gratification, his mind get's pure and is satisfied in the self. And a such is said to be in transcendence and pure consciousness."

Now, giving up does not mean, we can step doing work, we have to do it, not to satisfy our self but to please Krishna.

The person whose mind is not disturbed by any situation. Who is freed from attachment, fear or anger is said to be of a steady mind.

The person who remains as it is by whatever ups and downs that come into his life, who either praise them nor insults is said to be in perfect knowledge.

One should always be in a consciousness of the eternal Servant of Krishna and should carry on his duties for Krishna. Such a person is never affected by the three modes of material nature

Just as a tortoise withdraws its legs within its shell after seeing any danger, one should withdraw his sense from sense enjoyments as they are nor less than danger causing more material bondage.

One should engage himself, in the loving devotional service of Krishna and by doing so he will experience a higher taste. We always think that the material enjoyments are everything but a devotee of Krishna enjoys way more than a worldly person.

But, it is not so easy to control one's senses as they are very powerful. They could even carry away the mind of a person constantly desiring to control them.

When a person is being controlled by his senses, he has no control over himself. He cannot restrain himself from doing the wrong things.

But the one who fixes his mind on Krishna, controlling his senses and engaging in the devotional service is said to be a man of steady intelligence - by Krishna.

Now, Krishna will explain how a person falls down in this material world.

When a person contemplates with the Sense objects in this world, he gradually develops an attachment for them. This attachment is slowly converted into lust and the person desperately wants to enjoy that object. When this lust is not fulfilled, anger arises from it

When, he is angry, he falls into illusion and in illusion he would not be able to differentiate between the right and wrong. And such a person eventually falls down.

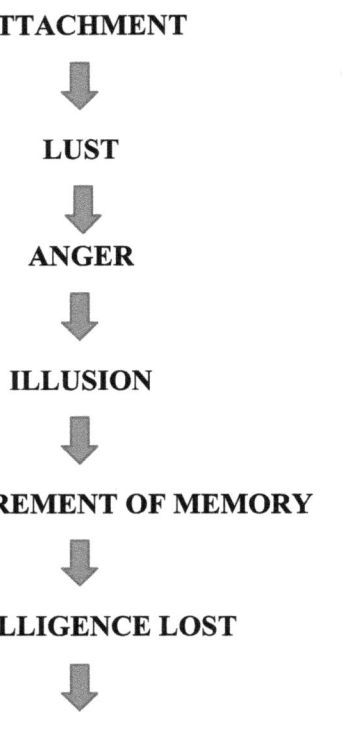

So, the stages of fall down

ATTACHMENT
⬇
LUST
⬇
ANGER
⬇
ILLUSION
⬇
BEWILDEREMENT OF MEMORY
⬇
INTELLIGENCE LOST
⬇
FALL DOWN

So, one should keep himself in content from the first stage which is attachment.

Such a person who is free from attachment and keeps his senses in Control can attain the full mercy of Krishna

And such a devotee of the Lord is not affected by the miseries in the world and he is satisfied. In this stage, his intelligence is established in Krishna consciousness.

From all this, we can understand that this material world is just like a house of miseries. The more, we are attached to something, the more we feel unsatisfied. And there can't be happiness without satisfaction.

And the only way to contain peace is to engage in the devotional service of Krishna. Krishna is the source of bliss and happiness from him rather than this material world which is the house of miseries.

As a boat is swept away by strong winds in the ocean, similarly, attachment to senses can take away ones intelligence.

Therefore, one should restrain himself from sense objects and just work as a matter of duty.

Krishna said: "what seems night to normal living entities is time of waking up for self-controlled person. And the time of waking up for all living beings is night for such persons.

As we are living, in this material world, we are full of desires in us. One cannot desire less. Even the want to be desire less is a desire in itself. But the one who controls this flow of desires within himself and engage in devotional service attains peace. Rather the person who goes mad, so much attached to his desire.

The key to real peace is to be free from all our desires. Who does not think himself as the doer or owner of everything but just a servant of the Lord.

And the one who lives a life like this is and remember Krishna at the hour of death can enter into his kingdom.

Chapter Three
"Karma Yoga"

We all have some **false ego** within us, which makes us think that **'I am the doer.** But actually it is not what we are doing. It is the **Supreme Lord: Krishna** who is **doing everything**. In this chapter Krishna will talk about **what is karma** actually.

Arjun asked Krishna: "O Krishna, why do you want me to **engage** in **fruitive work (karma),** if you think **intelligence is better than karma?"**

We often get the question that **why should we do karma?**

Krishna says that there are **two types** of men who try to realize self. One by practicing Sankhya or gyan yoga (Saint or knowledge) and the other by karma without devotional service.

This does not mean that one has **to stop doing karma**. It means we have to do it but at the **same time, not get attached to fruits of it.**

Whatever **we do is Karma**, everyone has to **act helplessly.** Even by **not doing anything,** one does Karma. This is due to the qualities obtained by the there modes of material nature. [goodness, passion and ignorance].

The person who **shows off** that he is not **attached to the senses** but whose **mind** is always **Fixed upon** those sense objects is said to be a Pretender in bold.

On the other hand, if a **sincere person** tries to control his senses and not get attached to it (in Krishna consciousness) is far **more superior.**

When your senses **are in control,** you are capable of doing anything.

Instead of **not doing anything**, Krishna supports to do your **prescribed duties without expectation.** Even mainting this body is impossible without doing work.

The work which is done as a sacrifice for Krishna, which is being offered to Krishna has to be done. Otherwise, other work causes budge or connection to this material world.

Whatever we do, one should offer it to Krishna. Thus, we will be free from attachment. Of this material world.

When we offer our work to demigods they would be pleased and prosperity will regin for all. They would give us happiness. But the person, who in return of this happiness does not offer his work to demigods is certainly a thief.

The devotees of the lord are free from all kinds of sins as they eat food which is offered to Krishna Prasad. Otherwise, the one who eats food only for his personal sense enjoyment, only for living certainly eats Sin. Therefore, one should avoid such food which cannot be offered to the lord.

Regulated activities for living entities are prescribed in the Vedas. The Vedas are directly the source of the supreme personality of Godhead.

Krishna says that one who does not live a human life as prescribed in the Vedas certainly lives a Life of sin. The Living entities who live only for the satisfaction of Senses live a life of Sorrow.

Because, the more we have the desire of sense enjoyments, the more we have expectations. And when those expectations are not fullfilled, they will give us sorrow.

On the other end, the one who takes pleasure in self, who lives for truth or self, who lives for truth or self-realization and who is satisfied in self. For him there is no duty.

This self-realization comes from Krishna consciousness.

A self-realized man has no duty to be performed, nor he has the reason to perform such duties. He is also not dependent on any other living being.

Therefore, one should do karma without getting attracted to the fruits of it. we should fulfill Karma as a matter of duty. By doing so, one attains supreme (Krishna).

Krishna further explains that, "O Arjuna, I am the Supreme personality of Godhead, there is no work prescribed for me. Nor I have the need to obtain anything, yet I am engaged in prescribed duties."

There is no other big leader than Krishna, he does not have the need to obtain anything, yet he does karma.

So, in order to live worldly life in Krishna Consciousness one has to end the selfishness within him and follow karma-yoga.

As Krishna is the leader, we all follow him. And if Krishna failed to engage carefully in karma, then we all would have not followed him.

Which would cause unrest in the world. Therefore, one should his duties without expectations and attachments.

Therefore, being the supreme Lord even Krishna does Karma without attraction. And we have to do the scene.

A person who has learned the real form of the Lord, who is full of knowledge should set an example for others. It is his duty to teach others to go on the path of Krishna Consciousness.

The soul who is filled with false ego thinks that he is the doer but he is actually carried by the three modes of material nature.

[goodness, passion & ignorance]

The one who is in knowledge of the absolute truth does not engage himself on senses and does not do karma for the gratification of senses. He understands the difference between work in frutive results and work in devotion [for Krishna] and work in frutive results.

Krishna says; "therefore. O Arjuna, Surrender all your work unto me, without thinking of gain or loss, victory or defeat and happiness or distress."

Those men who execute their duties according to Krishna's instructions are free from the bondage of material activities are eligible for liberation [moksha].

But the men of false ego, Listen to this knowledge and do not follow it are considered berefit of all knowledge.

Krishna says that everyone has a nature according to which they work. Even the souls full of knowledge work according to their nature.

The senses try to attach us to this material world. One should not come under the Control of his senses as they are great obstacles in the path of devotion.

One should perform his own prescribed duties and not follow other's duties.

Even if a person does his duties imperfectly. Still, he shall not do other's work. Destruction caused by one's own duty is better than engaging in other's duty.

Arjun asked: "O Krishna, then why do humans, unwillingly do sinful acts; as if engaged by force?"

Krishna replied: "It is lust only, Arjuna, which arises out of material world and later transforms itself into anger or wrath. One should treat lust and anger as his greatest enemy. "

As fire is covered by smoke, mirror is covered by dust, embryo is covered by womb. Similarly, a living entity covered by different degrees of lust.

Lust and anger are the main Obstacles in the path of Krishna consciousness.

And cause all the sinful reactions.

This lust is never satisfied and burns like fire which covers one's real knowledge.

The senses, the mind and the intelligence are the houses and the Sitting place of this lust. The lust covers them all and the living entity lives in ignorance.

Therefore, one should control his senses first in order to control his mind and lust.

Krishna further says "The senses are greater than body, the mind is greater than senses, the intelligence is greater than mind and the soul is greater than intelligence."

Therefore learn to know the mind and intelligence which will lead to knowing the soul.

Chapter Four
"Transcendental Knowledge"

Who is Krishna? Krishna is that supreme Lord. He is superior to all. He knows everything and everything is known to him. He was, is, and will always be there in all situations, in this chapter he will give us the divine knowledge with which we can understand him.

He says that this imperishable absolute knowledge was first instructed to the sun- god, Vivasvăn, and then to many the Father of mankind]. Later Manu instructed it to Iksvāku. But later on, this chain was broken and therefore this knowledge appears to he lost.

This very ancient science of relationship with the supreme is being Krishna's told to Arjuna by Krishna because he is very dear devotee and friend. And he can understand this transcendental mystery of science Krishna can do anything for his devotee.

Arjuna asked: "O lord, the sun-god vivasvan is older to you by marry birth.

Then how can I suppose to understand that you gave this knowledge to him?"

"The Supreme Personality of Godhead said: "O Arjuna, you and I have gone through many births but the difference is that you have forgotten them and I Still remember all"

Although, Krishna is unborn, and his transcendental body never deteriotes and he is the supreme lord of all living entities. Yet, his appears is millennium after millennium in his original transcendental form.

Whenever and wherever, there is a decline in religious practice and rise in irreligion. He descends himself.

To deliver the pious and to kill the miscreants, he appears himself millennium after millennium. But, his main motive is to protect his devotees and spend time with them.

One who knows the mystery behind his transcendental appearance. Knows that he is unborn. Upon leaving his body that person does not come to this material world but attains is eternal abode,

One who is free from attachment, fear and anger, who walks on the path of Krishna's teachings; who takes refuge under him experiences his transcendental Love for sure.

All those who surrender to Krishna, he rewards them according to the level of surrender. But everyone follows his path in all respects.

People of this world worship the demigod as they want success from frutive work. And they, of course, quickly get the result of the frutive work.

The Four divisions of the society are created by Krishna according to the three modes of material nature. But one should understand him as the noncreator.

There is no work that affects Krishna, nor does he desire for the fruits of the action. Those who understand this truth of him do not become entangled in the fruits of their work.

All liberated souls from the past times have followed this path of devotional service. This, in order to attain moksha, one should Follow their paths.

Even the most intelligent men in the world get confused between what is action and what is inaction.

Now Krishna will explain what actually Karma or action is, knowing which, one shall get liberated from all misfortune.

Karma is very complicated thing to understand. Therefore it is divided into three parts:

Action, Inaction and Forbidden action.

One should understand all of them. The person who is engaged in all sorts of material activities, but sees and inaction in action and action in inaction is known to be in his transcendental position.

What is inaction in action? Well, it means to do your work as a matter of duty and to not think yourself as the doer under the influence of false ego.

One who does work being unattached to the fruits of that work is said by sages to be a worker whose work is burned by the fire of perfect knowledge.

Abandoning all attachment from the results, to be independent and controlled, he is said to have done no work by doing every material activity.

Such a man whose mind and intelligence are in his full control acts only for the have bare necessities of life. He does not have ego and is not affected by sinful reactions. Such a worker works only for the necessaries to live a life.

One who is satisfied by whatever he obtains from his work, who is not envious or jealous of others; who is constant in both success and failure, is never entangled, although performing all activities.

The man whose work is unattached to the three modes of material nature and who is fully situated in transcendental knowledge devotion towards Krishna merges entirely into the transcendence .

A person who is in full Krishna consciousness to sure to attain his spiritual Kingdom due to his contribution to the absolute.

One should do all his work [prescribed duties] and simply depend upon Krishna. This way he offers it to Krishna and attains is eternal abode.

Fire can burn up anything. Similarly, some self-realized persons offer their actions to the fire of mental control, while the other ones in the material sense enjoyment offer their actions to fire of senses.

One who is interested in achieving self-realization can do it with a controlled mind full of knowledge. This knowledge can help us choose between the right and wrong.

Everyone has their own ways to walk on the path of self-realization, some do it by offering sacrifices to their possession, others by practicing Yoga, etc. One should know this path and try to implement it..

All those who know the meaning of this become cleansed of sinful reactions. And they advance towards the supreme eternal atmosphere. Without sacrifice, one can never lead a happy life on this planet.

All different types of sacrifices are mentioned in the Vedas. Some of them are told by Krishna himself; such as: Control your Senses and mind; be constant of tolerance-to every situation knowing these sacrifices and implementing them, one becomes liberated.

The sacrifice performed in knowledge devotional service is better is the mere sacrifices of material possessions. As all of them lead to transcendental position.

One should approach a spiritual master who is a self-realized man who can help us with understanding this knowledge given in Bhagavad Gita

Having obtained real knowledge from a spiritual master, one can never fall into illusion, for this you will see that all living entities are a part of the supreme, or in other words, they are of Krishna [the Supreme Lord].

Even if you are the most sinful person of the world but if you are in the boat of this transcendental knowledge. You will be able to cross the ocean of miseries.

This does not mean that you can do sins and then listen to the knowledge. Krishna tells that if you have done the most sinful act and are in the guilt that you won't be able to attain his eternal abode, can still do devotional service and attain Krishna's abode.

Just as fire burns up firewood into ashes, the fire of knowledge will burn all reactions to the material activities.

In this world, there is nothing more sublime and pure than transcendental knowledge. And one who is accomplished in pure devotional service enjoys this knowledge in due course of time

A man who is faithful and is dedicated to transcendental knowledge is eligible for attaining spiritual peace.

On the other hand, an ignorant or faithless man who doubts this knowledge falls down and there is no happiness for him. Neither in this world, nor in the next.

One who acts in devotional service, who renounces all his work by karma- yoga and whose doubts have been destroyed by transcendental knowledge is fully- situated in the self. And he is not bounded by reactions of his work.

Therefore, Krishna Says:

"Finish all the doubts with the Fire of Transcendental knowledge. O'Arjuna, stand and fight."

Chapter Five

"Karma-yoga. - Action in Krishna Consciousness"

In this chapter Krishna explains that in order to follow karma-yoga one should outwardly perform all actions and inwardly deny the fruits of it in order to be renounced. One should give all the fruits of his work to Krishna in in devotional service.

Arjuna asked: "O Krishna you first tell me to renounce all work (giving upwork) and again you are telling me to work with devotion. O Lord which of the two ways is better?"

The Supreme personality of godhead replied: "Both the ways are good for liberation But instead of becoming renouncing all work, working with devotion or devotional service is better as it is easier and everyone can do it."

A Sanyasi is not the one who wears orange coloured cloths and begs for food.

But a person who neither hates or desires the fruits of his action is said to be renounced. A person who is neither too happy upon receiving good fruits and nor too sad upon receiving bad fruits is freed from all the dualities of life. And such a person, Overcomes material bondage and is completely liberated.

One who thinks that gyan yoga and devotional service are two different paths is considered to be a fool.

An intelligent person is the one who thinks that by either of the ways one can attain benefit of both.

A person who just renounces all his activities but is not engaged in the devotional service of the lord cannot be happy. Krishna here tells the importance of devotional service, that a person who is engaged in devotional service can achieve the supreme without delay.

One who is a pure soul, who thinks that he is not the doer by controlling his mind and senses is dear to everyone and everyone are dear to him. Though he is always working, such a person is never entangled in material desires.

A person in divine consciousness, although engaged in Seeing, hearing, touching, Smelling, eating, sleeping and breathing is actually different from a normal person as while doing so, he does not think himself as the doer and thinks that only the material Senses are engaged with these objects and he is aloof from them.

One who performs duty without attachment who surrenders his work to the Supreme, does not incur any sinful reaction, as a lotus flower remains untouched with water.

Krishna here tells to be like a lotus, Stay in the dirt, but don't let the dirt touch you. One should be engaged in all sorts of activities but should remain unaffected by the results of it.

A yogi, abandoning all attachment, -works with all kinds of senses, but only for the purification (advancement in devotional Service or Krishna Consciousness).

A devoted soul attains peace as he Surrenders the results of his activities to Krishna, whereas, one who is not in union with divine and is greedy for the fruits of Lust actions becomes entangled.

When a person controls his nature and mentally renounces all actions, resides happily in the city of nine gates [the material body] neither working nor causing the work to be done.

A person who is master of the city of his body, does not create activities, nor does he induce people to act, nor does he create the fruits of his actions. He just surrenders it to the Lord...

However, when a person is enlightened with Knowledge, then his knowledge reveals everything to him as the sun lights up everything in the daytime.

But, to do this one should always be eager to learn something new. But when a person is fully lost in this material world, he does not sense anything beyond it, he does not recognize himself as soul or servant of Krishna and his real knowledge is covered by ignorance.

When one's intelligence, mind and faith are fixed upon the supreme. Such a soul is fully cleaned and walks straight on the path of liberation and devotional service.

One who is full of knowledge like the humble sages sees no difference between a cow and a dog. He sees everything and everyone equally (he sees everyone as a servant of Krishna)

Those whose minds are established in sameness and equality have already conquered conditions of birth and death. [They don't affect him]. Such a soul is said to be of full of knowledge.

A person who is neither too happy on achieving something pleasant, nor too sad on obtaining something unpleasant, who is self-intelligent is already situated in the transcendence.

We always look for pleasure in this material world. But Krishna says that all the miseries arise from the material sense pleasure. But the person who is full of knowledge is not attracted to material pleasures.

He just enjoys the happiness within himself. In this ways, the self-realized person enjoys unlimited pleasure as he concentrates on the Supreme, And this can be done rendering loving service to the supreme Lord.

An intelligent person does not take part in this material pleasure. As he understands that they have a beginning and an end. But the spiritual pleasure or the pleasure from within is unlimited and endless.

This does not mean we can stop doing karma. To live everyone has to act helplessly. We have to do Karma and offer it to Krishna.

Krishna further says that before leaving this present body, if one is able to tolerate and control his senses, then such a person is happy, in this world.

One who always tries to find happiness within is liberated in the supreme and ultimately, attains the supreme

Those who have ended up all material desires from within. Who just acts as a matter of duty for the welfare of all living things, who is free from all kinds of sins achieves liberation in the Supreme.

One who has controlled his senses, who is self-realized and self-disciplined and is constantly endeavoring for perfection is assured to get liberation in the near future.

Shutting out all external pleasures and keeping the eyes and vision concentrated between the eyebrows. Try to concentrate on inward and outward breath.[pranayama] This will help get free from desire, fear and anger. And one who is in this state is certainly liberated.

Krishna says a person who is in full consciousness of me, knowing me to be the supreme God and cause of all causes and the proprietor of everything is very very dear to me end and will attain me. And he will be freed from material miseries.

Chapter Six
Dhyana Yoga

In this chapter, Krishna tells us about Astanga – Yoga, a mechanical meditative practice which controls the mind and senses and focuses on the concentration of the Supreme.

The Supreme Personality of the Godhead said: "The person who does not desire the Fruits of his actions and only does the right Karma is said to be the real yogi."

Not the person who says that I have renounced all sorts of Karma. One should renounce the fruits of actions, not the action…"

One cannot become a Yogi or line oneself with Supreme unless he renounces the desires for fruits or sense gratification.

One needs to be in this world; perform all sorts of right karma, but be unattached to the fruits of it.

A person is said to be elevated in Yoga when, he renounces all material desires and neither acts for sense gratification nor engages in furtive work. He just does it as a matter of duty.

If you think that others can do you good and bad then that is wrong. You [your mind] alone are your biggest friend and enemy. Mind is the most difficult to control.

Krishna further says: "One must deliver himself by controlling his mind. For him, who has conquered mind, it is his best friend, and for him, who has failed to do so, his mind will remain the greatest enemy."

For one who has conquered the mind, the supreme soul [Krishna] is already reached. To such a man happiness and distress, heat and cold, honor and dishonor are all the same.

Krishna says that such a person is said to be independent as he has the control on the self…when we cry or be happy due to others or the current situation, we are dependent. Bu who has control on self will be calm and silent in all the situation.

He will only react when needed.

A person is said to be established in self-realization when he is completely satisfied by the knowledge he received. He is situated in the transcendence and is self-controlled. He sees no difference in sand and gold.

He sees everyone equally and does not differentiate between good and bad.

He loves everyone, even his enemies.

A transcendentalist should always engage his body, mind and senses on the Supreme, he should live alone in a secluded place from sometime and think of the lord. He should be free from desires and feelings of possessiveness. He should not have the attitude that everything is mine. He should see all the things as a property of Krishna, the supreme lord.

Krishna said: "To Practice Astanga yoga, one should go to secluded place and should lay kusa grass or aasana on the ground. This seat be neither too low nor too high. The person then should sit on it very firmly and practice Yoga to purify the heart by controlling senses and fixing the mind on one point."

"Then he should hold his neck, body and heat erect in a straight line and stare steadily at the tip of nose. One should be in a state of celebacy; Free from fear, without twinking anything, he should then meditate upon Krishna with all his heart and think of him as the ultimate goal of life."

Thus, after constantly practicing Astanga yoga by the control of body, mind and activities, one attains the eternal abode of Krishna. (This system is only for Brahmacharis).

There is no possibility of becoming a yogi if one eats too much or does not eat anything; or sleep too much or not sleep.

One should do every activity in a controlled manner or how much it is required to practice yoga.

One who performs every activity such as eating, sleeping, working in a manner can remove all material pains by practicing yoga.

When one controls his mental activities and becomes situated in the transcendence, away of all material desires, he is said to be perfect or well established in yoga.

As a lamp in a windless place does not waiver, similarly the controlled mind of a transcendentalist remains always steady by practicing yoga. He is always calm.

In the stage of perfections of yoga called trance or samādhi one's mind is completely restrained from material mental activies. He performs them but still is away or detached from them.

This perfection is characterized by one's ability to rejoice in the self, to find pleasure in self-realization. [Realizing oneself as the devotee of Krishna]

If you are not able to control the mind in the starting then don't fear, one becomes perfect by continuously practicing it. In this state of perfection [trance] one is bounded by unlimited transcendental happiness which is away from material desires.

Established thus, one never departs from the truth. Upon gaining it, he thinks there is no greater gain. Being situated, one in never shaken, even in between greatest difficulty. This is actual freedom from all miseries that arise from this material world.

In this world, yoğa is the only thing that will help us understand the absolute truth. It is the supreme happiness as it connects us with the lord.

One should engage himself on the path of yoga meditation and should not get distracted from it. He should abandon, without expectation al material desires and control this senses.

Step by step, one should become situated in the trance by means of intelligence and should focus on self alone and not think about anything.

The mind is very sensitive thing, it keeps wandering and thinking about things you don't want to do due to its unsteady nature. One should withdraw it back under the Control of self.

Krishna further tells that the yogi whose mind is fixed on him achieves the highest perfection of transcendental happiness. He is freed from all material contamination and reaction from the past deeds.

A true yogi observes Krishna in everything. He sees Krishna in all beings and all beings in Krishna. For those who see him everywhere, he is never lost, nor they are lost to him.

Such a yogi who engages in the worship devotional service of the Super soul, knowing that Krishna and super soul (Krishna's form situated in our heart) sees Krishna under all circumstances.

He is a perfect yogi who sees true equality in all living beings.in their happiness and even in their distress.

There often comes a question that if God exists why we cannot see him?

Krishna gives the answer here. The highest state of consciousness is in a devotee. One who performs devotional service and becomes situated in the trance can see God everywhere.

Arjuna asked, "O Madhusūdana, the system of yoga which you have prescribed seems impractical to meas the mind is very restless and unsteady."

"It is easy to say to be calm in both happiness and distress but I ask you how to bring that equality. How to control the restless mind?"

The Supreme Personality of Godhead said: "O son of Kunti, it is undoubtedly very difficult the control this restless mind, but it can be done by suitable practice and detachment."

Lord Sri Krishna is telling that with practice anything is possible with constant practice of yoga and devotional service one can control the mind.

Arjuna again asked "what is the path of an Unsuccessful transcendentalist? If one has started the practice of yoga but in the middle he stops it due to the materialistic mind. What will he do then? Will he get destroyed?"

"O Lord, please answer my question as there is no one else to answer it." Arjuna here accept Krishna as the only who can answer his questions.

The Supreme Personality of the Godhead answered: "O Arjuna, a transcendentalist engaged in the practice of yoga for the welfare of his soul does not meet with destruction, even neither in this word, nor in the Spiritual world, even though he is unsuccessful!"

Krishna tells that who does well, is never overcome by evil.

An unsuccessful yogi, after his death lives a life of enjoyment in heaven and after many years he is born in a family of righteous people. Who are transcendentalists, Who are great in wisdom And such a birth is rare in this world. Even after going to heaven, one has to come back in this world again. After taking such a birth, he receives divine consciousness from his previous life, and again tries to make further progress in yoga or devotional service to achieve complete Success and go to the abode of Krishna.

By the virtue of divine consciousness, he automatically becomes attached to Yogic principles, even without seeking them.....

When you follow Krishna's path, it will only give you profit.

Krishna further tells that when that yogi again engages himself in the practice of devotional services desiring for perfection, being washed of all material Contaminations, achieving perfection in yoga birth after birth, he finally attains the perfect supreme goal.

A yogi is greater than ascetic, greater than empiricist and greater than the than frutive worker. Therefore under all circumstances one has to be a yogi.

And of all yogis the Bhakti Yogi who abides in Krishna, thinks of him within and renders. Transcendental loving service to him - is most most intimately united with Krishna and is highest of all

Here, it is confirmed by Krishna, that of all yogas, be it Sankhya Yoga, karma Yoga, Asanga Yoga, etc. Bhakti yoga or Devotional service is the highest- of all.

Chapter Seven
"Knowledge of the Absolute"

In this chapter lord Krishna tells us about the actual knowledge. The advanced souls surrender unto him and impious souls divert their minds and worship other objects. Here he tells about who actually he is.

The Supreme Personality of. Godhead said: "O. Arjuna, by Practicing yoga, in full consciousness of me, with your mind attached to me, you shall know me in Truth without any doubt."

"I shall now give you this knowledge about knowing me."

Here comes this question that why is Krishna telling about his known good qualities? But he is telling this not out of ego but out of love so that Arjuna can be successful in whatever he does as Krishna loves his devotees very much. Because after knowing god, there is nothing else to be known.

There are thousands of men who worship Krishna. Out of those thousands one desires for perfection by practicing yoga, or devotional service and out of those who have achieved perfections hardly one knows Krishna in truth.

Krishna further explains: wind, air, water, fire and ether (gross elements) and mind, intelligence and False ego [subtle elements], through which the world is made. Together these eight constituents are my separated material energies. All of these are the inferior energies of Krishna.

Besides these, there is one more superior energy of Krishna which is comprised of all living entities. Which is One should not only See Krishna as Devaki - Nandan, Vrindvan vasi, Bansi Bajaiya but should also see him as one and the only absolute truth.

Krishna further tells that all the things come either from the material or the spiritual world. But he alone is the origin and dissolution of both the worlds.

Everything comes from him and one day will go in him only.

There is no truth Superior or greater than Krishna. Everything rests upon him like pearls are strung on thread. Everything which we see and do not see is Krishna.

Now Krishna will tell about the most important science or his tatva.

He says, "O Arjuna, I am the taste of water, the light of sun and moon, the syllable Om in Vedic mantras, the Sound in ether and the ability in man. I am the intelligence of the intelligent and proves of powerful man."

"I am the original fragrance of this earth, the heat in the fire, the lives of all that lives and penances of ascetics. I am the Original seed of all existences."

"I am the Strength of the strong, devotional or away of passion and desire; I am the sex life [according to scriptures]."

So, every right karma which is prescribed by the scriptures is Krishna.

He further tells that all States of being either goodness [satvik], passion [rajsik] or ignorance [tamsik] are Krishna's manifested energy, but he is independent. All three Modes of material nature come from him, but he is beyond them. These three modes affect us in this would, but they cannot affect the Lord or his pure devotees as they are always in transcendence.

These three modes of material nature goodness, passion and ignorance make up the illusion [Maya] in which, the entire universe is entangled.

Deluded by them the world doesn't know Krishna, who is beyond them we are always so much entangled in these true modes that we do not want to know Krishna.

One cannot know the form of Krishna until he has overcome the three modes.

Because where these three modes end, the science of knowing Krishna.

Krishna says that this divine energy of his consisting of the three modes is difficult to overcome, but one who has surrendered to him can easily cross it.

But the fools of material world whose knowledge is stolen by illusion do not surrender to Krishna. As they are bounded by their false ego and think that everything is mine.

Four kinds of people worship Krishna. The distressed, those who seek for money, the inquisitive or curious, and one who is searching for knowledge of the absolute truth.

By worshipping Krishna, they don't do a favour on Krishna but do a favour on themselves.

Out of these four one who seeks for knowledge, rendering pure devotional service to Krishna is the best. Krishna is very dear to him and he is very dear to Krishna.

All these four kinds of devotees are no doubt very divine souls. But the one who seeks knowledge in Krishna, he considers that person as his own self.

He who is situated in the transcendental loving service of Krishna is sure to attain him.

After passing through many births and deaths, he who is in actual knowledge, surrenders to Krishna knowing him as the primeval cause of all causes and such a soul is very rare and divine.

Those whose intelligence is stolen by material desires worship the demigods and follow the rules of worship according to their natures.

Krishna says that he is present in everyone's heart as the super soul.

Whenever a person wants to worship any demigod, Krishna makes his faith steady so that he can worship that particular demigod.

When he devotes to that demigod he would receive the benefits according to that deity's rules.

You can worship any other demigod other than Krishna, but the benefits you receive are bestowed by Krishna only.

But the men of small intelligence worship the demigods whose fruits are temporary. Those who worship them will go to their planets respectively.

But Krishna's devotees with ultimately reach his supreme planet. And the way to worship Krishna rendering pure devotional service to him.

Men of Small intelligence think of Krishna, the Supreme Personality of Godhead as an ordinary human being. Due to their small knowledge they don't know about his high nature and that he is imperisible they do not know that he is unborn and infallible. For them Krishna is covered by his internal potency [illusion].

But the intelligent men know about the real form of Krishna

One should therefore, worship Krishna as he is the supreme Personality of Godhead and all the demigods work under him.

The Supreme Personality of Godhead further said: "I know all the things that had happened in the past, all the things that are happening in the present, and all the things that will happen in the future. I know all the living entities. But no one knows me".

Krishna explains that all living entities are born into delusion and bewildered by attraction arisen from desire and hate.

So, in order to surrender and love Krishna, one should finish all the material desires he has from the heart.

People who have done pious acts in previous birth and this and whose sins are removed are free from the illusion and they engage themselves in Krishna's devotional service with determination.

Krishna never said to leave your karma. He Says to do all right work, but to not expect any fruits from it. In this way one becomes liberated from the endless cycle of births and deaths.

A person who offers his work to Krishna, in the full consciousness of him. Seeing him in everyone. Knowing him to be supreme Lord is an actual Brahman and can remember him even at the time of death

Chapter Eight
"Attaining the Supreme"

S cience discovers something new daily... But even after thousands of years, the science behind Bhagavad-Gita hasn't changed. This chapter Krishna will talk about Brahman, Spirituality and work and how can one remember him at the time of his death.

Arjun asked:"O Supreme Lord, What is a Brahman? What is the self? What are Material manifestation? And what are demigods? What are frutive activities?

"And those who are in your pure devotional service how are they able to remember you at the time of death. Please explain these to me".

Arjun here is curious about this and wants Krishna to answer his questions.

Krishna now answers these questions.

He says that the indestructible living entity is the Brahman and his eternal nature is spirituality, the self. Knowing the soul and super soul is Spirituality. And actions performed for Sense gratification for development of the material body are frutive activities.

Then he further says that the things which are physical, and constantly changing are called adhibhuta, which is the whole world. The universal form of lord, which includes all the demigods is called adhidaiva. And Krishna, who is situated as the Supersoul in the heart of all living entities is the adhiyagna.

One should offer his every work to Krishna and engage in the devotional service of Krishna. By doing so he can remember him at the time of death.

Those who remember Krishna at the time of death attains his eternal abode, without any doubt. A person's life is like a saving account, his work or Karma either good or bad is stored in his account. And whatever State of being he remembers at the time of death. He will attain that in his next birth.

Therefore Krishna says to Arjuna that he Should always think of him and at the same time carry out his prescribed duty.

With your activities dedicated to Krishna and your mind and intelligence fixed on him. You will even remember him at the time of death and are sure to attain him.

Therefore one should constantly meditate upon Krishna.

One should meditate upon the Supreme who Personality of Godhead as the one who knows everything, who is the oldest and the Controller, who is smaller than the smallest, who maintains everything... who is inconceivable, who is beyond the material creation.

One, who at the time of death, fixes his life air between the eyebrows and without any feeling of Lust or anger remembers Krishna with full devotion, is sure to reach him.

Krishna Further says that people who are learned in the scriptures and who are great sages in the renounced order enter into the Brahman state.

Now, Krishna will tell about the process of attaining liberation. :

A yogi should be free from all kinds of attachments and sensual pleasures. He should fix his mind on the heart and life air at the top of the head. And establish himself in yoga.

After being situated in yoga and uttering the syllable on, which is a combination of three spiritual letters, if one remembers Krishna and quits his body, he is sure to reach the Spiritual planets.

For who one who always remembers Krishna without deviation. Whose consciousness is always fixed upon Krishna will surely obtain Krishna due to his constant engagement in devotional Service.

One can think of Krishna as anything: as the supreme absolute truth, as father, son, brother, friend, lover, husband, etc.

After obtaining Krishna, the great souls, who are yogis never return to this material temporary world full of miseries, as they have attained the highest perfection.

In this material world, above our Planet are many higher planets and below, it are the lower planets. But all these planets, from higher to lower are full of miseries wherein, repeated births and deaths takes place. But those who attain Krishna's supreme abode will never come back to this material world.

We have four yugas namely - Satyayuga, Tretayuga, Dwaparyaga and Kalyuga. All there four yugas together form one mahayuga.

By human calculations, One thousand Mahayugas form Lord Brahma's one day. Same is the duration of his one night.

When Lord Brahma's day begins all living entities, this entire universe comes into existence. And when his night begins the entire universe is destroyed again.

But beyond this manifested and unmanifested [destructible] matter lies another abode which is eternal and is never destroyed, which is the supreme abode of Krishna. When the entire universe is destroyed, this abode of Krishna remains as it is.

That which the Vedantists describe as the unmanifest and infallible which the Supreme destination and having attained it, one never returns to this material world, is Krishna's abode.

Krishna, who is the supreme personality of Godhead can only be attained by unalloyed devotion. By loving service towards him.

Although he is there in everyone's heart as the super soul, he is present everywhere and everything is situated in him.

If Krishna talks about how to live a life, then he also tells how to die. He will now explain the circumstances, under which, if a yogi dies will not take a birth again.

He says that if a person leaves his body during the influence of fiery god, the light, at an auspicious moment. of the day, during the fortnight of the

waxing moon, or during the six months when the sun travels in the north attains the Supreme.

And the person who leaves his body during the smoke, the night, the fortnight waning moon, or the six months when the sun travels in the south reaches the moon planet and takes birth again.

So basically, there are two ways of passing from this material world one in light and another in the darkness. One who passes away in the light does not take birth again, but one who passes away in darkness, returns to this world.

Although devotees know these two paths and they are never distracted.

Therefore, always be fixed in devotion, towards Krishna.

A person who accepts the path of devotional service is not berefit of studying Vedas, performing austerities, giving charity or pursuing philosophical or frutive activities. Simply by performing devotional service he gets the benefit of all these and at the end reaches the Supreme abode.

Chapter Nine
"The Most Confidential Knowledge"

Lord Krishna is the supreme personality of Godhead and the supreme object of worship. We as a soul, are eternally connected to him. And the one who has attained his love has many spiritual opulence. In this chapter, Krishna will talk about all the opulence of a Yogi .He will also talk about the knowledge of self- realization. The knowledge give in this chapter is the Supreme of all knowledge.

Lord Krishna said: "My dear Arjuna, because you are never envious of me, I shall give you this most confidential knowledge and realization, knowing which you shall be freed from all material miseries."

The knowledge which Krishna is going to tell is the king of education, the most secret of all Secrets. It is the purest Knowledge and gives the direct perception of self by realization. It is everlasting and it is joyfully performed. Those who are not faithful or dedicated in his devotional Service cannot attain him. And they return to the endless cycle of birth and death.

By Krishna, in his unmanifasted form, this entire universe is pervaded. All Living entities are in him but he is not in them.

Just like water and ice.Ice is made up of water and water is present in every part of ice. But ice is not present in water.

Similarly, all matter (living or non-living) comes from Krishna and is present in him but he is all detached from them.

He is the maintainer of all living entities and is present everywhere. Yet he is not a part of this cosmic manifestation. And he is the source of creation.

We must understand that as the mighty wind, blowing uncontrollably, rests in the Sky, similarly all living entities rest upon Krishna.

Krishna further explains that at the end of one millennium, all material creations enter into his nature and at the beginning of another millennium, he creates them all again by his divine potency.

This whole cosmic manifestation is under Krishna. Under him it will be created and destroyed again and again.

Although he is never attached to these material activities and they cannot bind him.

He is seated as the neutral.

Even Krishna follows the rules created by him, though they cannot bind him.

And his duty is to control this material nature and under his order all beings [moving or non-moving] are created and annihilated. Or destroyed.

So if one thinks that he can do anything of his choice then it is wrong.

Krishna is the supreme controller of everything.

Fools cannot understand Krishna when he descends in human form. They do not know his transcendental nature as the Supreme Lord of all. They just see him as a human being due to their false ego.

Those who are of demonic and atheistic nature do not understand Krishna. In this Condition, the hopes for liberation, their frutive activities and their culture of Knowledge are all defeated.

But those who are of the divine nature are always engaged in devotional service of Krishna. And at the same time, they work welfare of other living beings.

Always chanting about the glories of the supreme Lord, bowing down to him, they always worship Krishna in devotion.

It is actually Krishna, who is the ritual, the sacrifice, the offering to the ancestors, the healing herb, the transcendental chant... He is the butter and fire in the offering. [yagna]

Krishna is the original father and mother of this universe. He is the object of knowledge and the syllable Om. He is the Rig, Sama and Yajur Vedas.

He is the goal, the sustainer, the master, the witness the supreme abode who everyone the seeks and the most dear friend Krishna is the creation and destruction on the basis of everything.

Krishna gives the heat and rain. He is the immortality and also the death personified, both spirit and matter lies in him.

From the above given explanation, we can understand that everything that is happening in this world is Krishna. Even if we think that we are doing something, it is Krishna actually who is doing everything.

Krishna further explains that the person who studies the Vedas and do pious. activities by seeking the heavenly planets; He sends them to heaven, [the abode of Indra] where they enjoy godly delights, or pleasures.

But after they have enjoyed all the sense Pleasures of their pious activities in the heaven, they will have to return to this mortal planet again.

Krishna is trying to say that those who do the right and pious work but are binded to the fruits of it surely go to heaven, but they will have to take a new birth again in this house of miseries.

But those who worship Krishna with pure devotional service and are not binded by the fruits of their action are rare souls and their responsibility is taken care by Krishna himself.

Krishna further explains that those who worship other gods indirectly worship him only. But they certainly do it in a wrong way.

All other demigods are the expansion of the supreme lord, Krishna himself.

And by pleasing Krishna all other demigods are pleased.

Therefore, one should worship the supreme Lord Krishna, under all circumstances. Krishna is the enjoyer and master of all sacrifices. And those who do not understand his transcendental nature fall down and take birth again.

Those who worship demigods attain them, those who worship the ancestors attain them, those who worship ghosts and Spirits take birth among them demigods.

But those who worship Krishna attain his Supreme abode. Therefore the devotees of Krishna never take birth again. It does not mean that Krishna and the demigods are the same. Krishna is the Supreme personality of Godhead. And all the demigods work under him. Krishna always sees our love towards him. Even if we offer a leaf, a flower or a fruit with love, he will accept it.

Whatever one does, whatever one eats or whatever one performs, one should do it as an offering to Krishna

In this way, he will not be bounded by the fruits of it and will be freed from the bondage of the work and with his mind fixed upon Krishna he gets liberated and attains Krishna.

Krishna envies no one, nor is he partial towards anyone. He loves everyone equally. But the ones who love him. back will be able to feel his love. And the people in the engaged in the material world will not understand his love.

As Krishna is not partial to anyone, even if the most sinful person in the world offers pure devotional service to Krishna, he will also be considered saintly.

That person quickly, becomes righteous and attains everlasting peace. Krishna says and boldly declares that it is his promise that his devotee never perishes.

Even if people of lower birth women – women [prostitutes], vaishya [merchants] and Sūdras [workers] take the shelter of Krishna, they will also attain his supreme abode.

Because for him everyone are equal and he is not partial to anyone.

Krishna says us to do four things –

Always think of him, become his devotee, worship him and offer your obeisance unto him. Being completely absorbed in him, you will surely come to him. Thus, always engage in his pure devotional Service.

Chapter Ten
The Opulence of the Absolute

As the chapters in the Bhagavad Gita proceed further, we are getting to know about Krishna's Tatva. Till now it is clear that all the things in the world [living or non-living] originate from Krishna himself. And he is the Supreme object of worship. In this chapter Krishna will tell us about his opulances and summaries the knowledge he has given in previous chapters.

The Supreme personality of God head said: "O Arjuna, you are my very dear friend, so listen again, I am giving you this knowledge which is better and easier than previous one for your benefit."

Neither the host of the demigods nor the great sages, in every respect know Krishna's origin or orpulances. He is the source of demigods and sages. All of them originate from him.

And one who knows that Krishna is unborn and beginingless, as the supreme Lord of all living entities, is freed from all kinds of sins.

Intelligence, knowledge, freedom from doubt and delusion, forgetfulness, truthfulness, control of the sense, control of the mind, happiness and distress birth, death, fear, fearfulness, non violence, equanimity, satisfaction, austerity, caring, fame and infamy – all these different qualities of living beings are created by Krishna himself.

So basically, Krishna is trying to summarize all the knowledge he has given till now for our better understanding.

Krishna further explains that before all the living entities existed, there were seven great sages, from whom we have come into existence.

And before these seven great sages existed. Four things —mind, intelligence, consciousness and fasle ego. But all of these come from Krishna.

Those who know about these opulances and power of Krishna, without a doubt engaged themselves in the unalloyed devotional service of Krishna.

The devotees of Krishna know that he is the source and dissolution of both material and spiritual worlds, and they worship him with all their hearts.

Krishna further describes the nature of his devotes and say that he is always dwelling in the thoughts of his devotees and their lives are fully surrendered to his devotional service and they are always conversing about him. They can do anything for the service of Krishna.

And to those who are constantly devoted to serving Krishna with love, he gives them the understanding to come back to him.

And to show them special mercy, he destroys the darkness born of ignorance from the minds of his devotees. He destroys all their illusion. And enlightens them with knowledge.

Arjuna said: "O Krishna, you are the Supreme personality of godhead, the ultimate truth, the purest, the supreme abode, the unborn, the greatest. You are eternal, transcendental and the original person."

"Great sages such as Narada, Asita, Devala and Vyasa have confirmed this truth about you and now you yourself are telling it to me."

"O Lord, I accept you as the Supreme absolute truth. Neither demigods, nor the demons know about your personality."

"You alone only know yourself by your internal potency, O lord of all living beings, O' God of Gods!"

"Please tell me in detail, about your divine opulence's by which you provide in this world."

"O krishna!, how I shall think of you, and how shall I know you? You appear and are to be remembered in various forms. Please tell me about your divine forms."

"Please again describe me about the mystic power of your opulences. I am never satisfied in hearing about you, the more you say, the more I want to hear and taste the nectar of your words."

The Supreme Personality of Godhead replied: "Yes, my dear Friend, I will tell about manifestations, but as my opulences are limitless and infinite. I will only tell you about the important ones."

Arjuna wants to know about the opulences of Krishna, but they are beyond human perception so Krishna will only about the important ones.

He further says: "I am the Supreme Soul seated in the heart of all living beings. I am the beginning, middle and end of all living entities."

"Out of the twelve Adityas, I am Vishnu, of lights, I am the Sun of the maruts, I am mrici, and among all the Stars, I am the moon."

"Of all the vedas, I am Samu Veda, and of demigods, I am Indra, out of the senses, I am mind and in all living beings, I am consciousness."

"Out of Rudras, I am Lord Shiva of Yakshas and Rakshasas, I am Kuvera [lord of wealth], of the Vasus I am Agni (fire) and out of the mountains, I am meru. Out of the priests, I am the chief one Brhaspati, of generals, I am Kartikeya, all and out of water bodies, I am the ocean."

"Out of the great sages, I am Bhrgu, of vibrations, I am the transcendental spiritual combination of Om. Of all sacrifices, I am chanting or japa of the holy names [Hare Krishna Hare Krishna Krishna Krishna Hare Hare/Hare Ram Hare Ram Ram Ram Hare Hare] and of the immovable things and am the Himalayas."

"Out of all trees, I am banyan tree, and of sages among the demigods, I am Narada of the Gandharvas, I am Citraratha and among perfected beings, I am sage Kapila."

"Of horses, know me as Uccainśrava, which was produced during chanting of the ocean for nectar. Of lordly elephants, I am Airavata and among men I am the King or Monarch."

"Of weapons, I am Vajra or thunderbolts, among cows I am Surabhi or Kamdhenu. Of causes of procreation, I am Kandrarpa, or god of love, and Serpents I am Vasuki."

"Out of many-hooded Wagas, I am Ananta Sesa, and among aquatics I am Varuna of departed ancestors, I am Aryama and of the dispensers of low I am Yama [god of death]."

Krishna is trying to explain that out of any field in life, he is its speciality.

He further continues: "among the daity demons, I am the great devotee Prahlada, out of subduers, I am time of beasts I am the lion and among birds I am garuda."

"Out of purifiers, I am the wind, of the wielders of weapons, I am Lord Rama, of fishes, I am shark and of the flowing rivers, I am the holy Ganges."

"Of all creations, I am the beginning, middle and end. Out of all sciences, I am the spiritual science of realization of self and among logicians I am the Conclusive truth."

"Among the letters, I am A, of compound words. I am the dual compound. I am the inexhaustible time and of creators, I am Brahma."

"I am the cause of birth and death among all living entities. Among women I am Fame fortune, fine speech, memory, intelligence, Steadfastness and patience."

"Out of the hyms of sama veda, I am the Br hat - sama and of poetry I am Gayatri. Among months I am the Magartira [November December], and of seasons I am spring."

"Of all the cheats. I am (Gambling) (Krishna has his specialty in every aspect of world. But it does not mean we could do wrong things). Of splendid, I am the splendor. I am the victory and adventure and the strength of the strong.

"Of the descendents of visni, I am Vasudeva and of the Pandavas, I am Arjuna, of the sages, I am Vyāsa and out of great thinkers, I am Usana."

"Among all means of suppressing lawlessness I am punishment and among those who seek victory, I am morality. Of Secret things, I am silence and of the wise, I am the Wisdom."

"I am the generating seed of all existences. Any being [moving non-moving] cannot exist without me."

This knowledge which Krishna gave to Arjuna was just a mere indication of his divine opulences. They are eternally Infinite.

All the beautiful, opulente and glorious things you see in this world are just a spark of Krishna's beauty.

But if Krishna has about some of his opulences it does not mean that we will worship those opulences. One should always worship the original form of the Lord as Krishna.

After reciting all this knowledge Krishna says to Arjuna that what is the need of all this detailed knowledge, when, with single fragments piece of his infinite opulences he controls and supports this entire cosmic manifestation or creation.

Chapter Eleven
The Universal Form

In this chapter Krishna will give Arjuna divine eyes, with which he could, see his Supreme Universal form which is unlimited. Krishna will explain that his divine humanlike form and that one can only see him with pure devotional service.

Arjuna Said: " O supreme Lord, you have showed your divine mercy by telling me about your transcendental and spiritual opulences. My illusion has been completely gone now."

"O' Lotus-eyed one, you have told me about appearance and disappearance of every living entity and have realized unlighted your glories."

"O my lord, though I know you in your actual form which you have described to me. But I want to see how you have entered this cosmic manifestation. I want to see your universal form. So my Lord if you think that I am able to manifest behold your divine unlimited form, then please kindly show your universal self."

After getting the divine knowledge from Krishna, Arjuna is a now very curious to know how millions of universes come from Krishna and dissolve in him.

The Supreme Personality of Godhead" Arjuna, my son, now see my unlimited opulences, hundreds and thousands of varied divine and multicolored forms."

Krishna's divine universal form is beyond our imagination. Au the things [living or non-living] manifest from his divine form.

He further said to Arjuna, "Now see the different manifestations of Adityas, Vasus, Rudras, Ashvini. Kumaras and all other demigods. Now see those wonderful things you haven't seen before. O Arjuna, whatever you want to see, whatever you have desired. is visible whatever in my universal self. Everything past, present, Future, moving, non-moving is here, at one place."

"But you cannot see my divine form with your present material eyes given by the three modes of material nature. Therefore, I give you divine eyes, to behold my mystic opulence".

Sanjaya said, "O King, after speaking these, the Supreme Personality of Godhead Showed Arjuna, his all-pervading universal Form"

Even Sanjaya was given with divine eyes so that he could describe what was going in the battle field of Kurekshetra.

After this you will read a description of the universal form of Krishna.

Whatever Krishna has said about him in the Bhagavad Gita, you will now read a practical description of what it looks like.

Arjuna saw in the universal form unlimited mouth, unlimited visions; unlimited eyes. The universal form, was decorated with various garlands and ornaments and beared many unlimited weapons. He wore celestial garments. Many divine scents or aromas came from the universal form. All of that was wonderful, beyond imagination, unlimited excellent and all expanding.

The light coming from the universal form looked as if hundreds of thousands of suns resembled in the sky at the same time.

Arjuna could also see many millions of universes being created and destroyed in the universal form. He could see different expansions of universe all at one place though divided into many thousands.

After then, astonished and bewildered, Arjuna bowed his hands and with folded hands began to pray to the Supreme Lord.

He said: "My dear Lord Krishna, I can various living entities and all the demigods being situated in your universal form. I can see Lord Brahma sitting on the Lotus flower. I can even see Lord Shiva and all other divine Serpents."

The universal form was so divine, unlimited and all expanding.

Arjuna continued praying and said that he could see in the body of to the lord of universe many arms, bellies, mouth and eyes expanded everywhere unlimitedly. He could see no beginning, middle and end of Krishna's universal form.

It is very difficult for Arjuna to describe Krishna's form in words. It is very difficult for him to see the universal form as the divine light coming from it is spreading in all directions. The light is like blazing fire or the immeasurable radiance coming from the sun. The glowing form is adorned with Various crowns, clubs and dises.

Arjuna says, "O Lord, you are the Supreme object of love and worship.

You are the ultimate resting place of all universe You are the oldest and maintainer of eternal religion. That is my opinion.

Anything and Everything in millions of universe rests upon Krishna.

Krishna's glory is unlimited. The universal form has countless arms. The sun and the moon are its eyes. Blazing fire is coming from its mouth, which is burning this entire universe by its own heat.

We have seen this earth, the things which are beyond this earth also. But imagine if you see all these things resting upon Krishna at one place. The universal form of Krishna is wonderful but at the same time terrible.

Different hosts of demigods surrendering and entering before Krishna. Some of them are very afraid offering prayers with folded hands. Hosts of great sages are crying and singing different vedic hymes into the universe form.

All the expansions of Lord Shiva, the Adityas, the vasus, the sadhyas, the viis vedevas the two Ashvis, the maruts, the forefathers The Grandharvas the Yakshus, the Asura and the perfected demigods are looking at Krishna in wonder.

All the planets along with the demigods are astonished of seeing Krishna's universal form with unlimited arms, legs, eyes, and bellies and countless terrible teeth. They are all disturbed and so is Arjuna.

Seeing the many radiant colours coming from the form of Krishna, which is touching the sky, Arjuna is disturbed with fear. He could no longer control the equilibrium of mind.

Normally after seeing Lord Krishna in Vrindavand or Dwarka, our mind gets peace. But the Universal form of Krishna was so terrible and horrified that even Arjuna could not stand on his feet.

Arjuna continued saying," O Lord of lords, please be gracious to me. I am not able to keep my balance seeing your deathlike faces and terrible teeth. I am bewildered in all directions."

"I can also see all so sons of Dhritrastra along with their allied kings including Bhishma, Drona and Karna entering into your head and getting crushed by your teeth."

All these great warriors are entering the mouth of Krishna as the rivers enter into the Ocean.

They are rushing in full speed as the moths dash in a blazing fire.

Krishna is devouring all people from all sides with his flaming mouths. It covering all with his effulgence. Its manifestations is terrible with scorching rays.

Arjuna requested, "O Supreme Lord, I offer my obesances unto you. Please have mercy on me. Tell me who you are, I want to know about you, I don't know what real mission is. Of my Lord please tell me."

Arjuna wanted to see the universal form of Krishna to fulfill his curiosity.

But after seeing it, he is now more curious to know about Krishna.

The Supreme Personality of Godhead said: "I am the time, the destroyer of all worlds. I have come here to destroy all the sinful people. Except you [the Pandavas], all the soldiers on both the sides will be killed."

This shows that even though Arjuna did not want to fight but the deaths of all of them were fixed by Krishna and all of the soldiers had to be all killed by Krishna's own will.

Krishna further said: "O Arjuna!, Therefore please get up and fight to win glory, after conquering your enemies you can enjoy a Kingdom flourishing. All of our opponents deaths are arranged by me and you are just an aid.

Even though Arjuna was scared to pick up his bow and fight against Drona, Bhishma and his family member, their deaths were arranged and fixed by the Supreme Authority, Krishna himself. Therefore Krishna asks him not to be disturbed and to simply fight.

Sanjaya said: " O King Dhritrastra, after hearing these words by the Supreme Personality of Godhead, a trembling Arjuna started to offer obeisance to Krishna with folded hands."

It is impossible for materially conditioned souls like us to even think of Krishna's universal form as we are so engaged in material entanglement.

Therefore after gaining some courage and strength, Arjuna spoke following words: No the Supreme one, the master of senses, the world is joyful by hearing your name and everyone are attached to you. The perfect souls offer obeisances and there respectful homage and demons, being afraid flee here and there. All of this is so rightly done."

"O Lord, you are even greater than the Brahman. You are the original creator.

And why should anyone not offer obeisances unto your lotus feet. As you are limitless, the invincible source, cause of all causes, the supreme enjoyer and proprietor. You are transcendental beyond, material contamination."

Arjuna has lost his senses after seeing Krishna's universal form. After controlling himself he addresses Krishna as the original Personality of Godhead as before the creation, in the creation and after the creation, he alone will exist.

Krishna is the ultimate sanctioner of everything happening in these worlds.

He is the knower of everything and he is all that is knowable which means that after knowing Krishna, there is nothing else to be known.

He is above this material creation and is transcendental. He is limitless.

Nothing can happen in this world, without his sanction in the world. Krishna is the air, the supreme control, the fire, the water, the moon. He is Brahma who is the first living Creature of this world and even the great-grandfather.

Arjuna is offering respectful obeisances a thousand times again and again.

He is offering obeisances to Krishna from all the directions. Krishna is the master and everything existing. He is all pervading and this entire cosmic manifestation has emerged from Krishna.

Arjuna further says:" O Lord not knowing about your glories I have addressed you O Krishna, O Yadava O my friend, many times thinking of you as a friend. I had done that in love and please forgive me for that. I have sat with you, we ate together and played also. I have dishonored you several times and please forgive me for my offenses."

Arjuna is trying to explain that Krishna is the father of millions of universes in these cosmic manifestation. He is the supreme spiritual master and no one is equal or superior to him. He is the lord of immeasurable power. No one can be compared to him.

He further says " O my lord, you are the supreme and are worshiped by every living entity. But please show your mercy upon me and as a father tolerates the wrong things of his son, a friend or a master tolerates many wrong things. Please tolerate the wrong things that I have done to you."

After seeing the universal form of Krishna, Arjuna is very happy. But at the same time his mind is also very disturbed. He asks Krishna to bestow his grace upon him and to reveal his form with helmeted head and club, wheel, couch and lotus flower in hands as the Personality of Godhead again. Actually, the two-handed form of the Lord is more transcendental and powerful than the universal form.

We all live in this material world which is also referred to as House of miseries by Krishna. We as souls are materially contaminated and we expect happiness from the material world. However we only get distress.

Therefore when Arjuna saw the real happiness which Krishna in his original form as the Supreme Personality of Godhead, he became very much pleased and is now asking the lord to come back again on the battlefield of Kurukshetra.

The Supreme Personality of the Godhead said: "O Arjuna, I have shown you this form very happily by my internal potency. This universal form is beyond the material world. Before you, one has seen this all-pervading, limitless form of mine".

Arjuna had seen the universal form of Krishna which no one could see neither by studying Vedas, nor by performing sacrifices by doing many pious activities.

He was very disturbed by seeing this horrible form of Krishna. Therefore, Krishna by his causeless mercy, showed him the four-armed form which he desired.

Sanjaya said to Dhritrastra: "O King, after having spoken this, the Supreme Lord showed his four-armed form and then two-armed form encouraging a fearful Arjuna".

When Arjuna saw Krishna in his four arm beautiful humanlike form, He is now very calm and has regained his original consciousness.

The Supreme Personality of Godhead said:

"My dear Arjuna, even the four armed form of mine which you are seeing now is very difficult for the demi gods to see and they are always seeking the opportunity to see this form."

This shows that Krishna is very merciful towards his devotees that he can even show his divine universal form.

The form which Arjuna was seeing with his transcendental eyes cannot be understood by studying the vedas, nor by undergoing severe penances, nor by Charity.

Krishna says that only by undivided devotional service one can understand him. Only by loving service one can understand the mysteries of Krishna's existence.

Krishna says:" O Arjuna one who engages himself in my devotional service, who is free from all material contaminations and mental speculation, he works for me and who dedicates his life unto my lotus feet, comes to me."

It is said then it is impossible to see the divine form of Krishna but one who always has this feeling for desire for Krishna can easily see Krishna everywhre

Chapter Twelve
Devotional Service

In the previous chapters, Lord Krishna has given very special importance to devotional service. It is also known as Bhakti yoga, in which one surrenders him and all his activities completely to Krishna. In this chapter, Krishna will explain about devotional service in detail, which is the highest form of yoga.

Arjuna asked: "O Lord, out of those who are constantly engaged in your devotional service and those who worship the impersonal brahman, who is said to be more perfect?"

So, Krishna has various potencies, one of his potencies is the all-pervading impersonal Brahman which does not have a form. But sometimes people think that God or Krishna does not, have a form However, that impersonal brahman is Just a potency or the divine light coming from the body of Krishna. So Arjuna here asks that out those who constantly engage themselves in Krishna's personal form and those who worship the impersnal brahman [no form] who is more perfect?

The Supreme Personality of Godhead Said;" those who fix their minds on my personal form and worship me with transcendental faith are considered to be most perfect."

Krishna here confirms that he is not formless, he does have a very beautiful humanlike form.

Krishna further explains that those who control their senses and desires. and worship the all-pervading, inconceirable, fixed and immovable impersonal brahman at last achieve Krishna only as it his potency, But those whose minds are fixed upon the impersonal Brahman feather of the supreme, spiritual advancement is very trouble some. They face many problems in their spiritual journey.

This has a Logic. when we worship the impersonal Brahman who does not have a form, there is no exchange of feelings, as it does not have a form and when we are fixing our minds upon the personal form of Krishna there is an exchange of feelings as we can offer him food, dance with him, etc.

Therefore Krishna says that worshiping the impersonal brahman comes with many problems and he [Krishna] does have a very beautiful form which we can worship.

Krishna further says that those who worship him, surrender all their work unto him and fix their mind and intelligence in Krishna and constantly practice devotional service, for them, Krishna acts as a deliverer from the ocean of birth and death.

So, in order to engage oneself the devotional service, one should fix their minds upon Krishna and engage all his intelligence in the Supreme personality of God head. Thus one will always live in Krishna without a doubt.

Krishna says:" My dear Arjuna, if you are not able to fix your minds upon me then follow the regulative principles of bhakti-yoga. In this way you will develop a desire for me."

There are four regulative principles described Krishna:

No Gambling

No meat Eating

No Intoxication

No Illicit sex

So basically, engage your senses in the Service of Krishna

If one strictly follows these four principles and chant Hare Krishna (yoga- system for kaliyuga), he win automatically develop a desire for Krishna.

And even if you cannot follow these basic principles of bhakti-yoga then Should simply work only and only for Krishna, as by working for Krishna, he will come on the perfect stage and will start following these principles.

If you are even not able to work in the consciousness of Krishna then just give up all the fruits of your actions and try to be self-situated.

If you are certainly not able to do this then just engage your mind in the cultivation of knowledge. Try to get more and more spiritual knowledge.

However, better than knowledge is meditation and beater than meditation is giving up actions.

Krishna has suggested every way in which a yogi can take to devotional service.

Krishna further says: "One who does not envy anyone and is always kind to everyone. Who does not think himself as the enjoyer or proprietor, free from false ego, and is self-situated, who remains equal in both happiness and distress satisfied who always engaged in the devotional services of me, Such a devotee of mine, is very dear to me."

Krishna here describes all the qualities of devotee which he likes. And even one who tries to achieve these qualities is very dear to Krishna.

He from whom no one is put into difficulty and no one is disturbed, he who treats both happiness and desires, fear and anxiety equal is very dear to Krishna.

One who does not have any expectations, who is pure, expert, without cares, free of any all pains and who does not have any ambition for material enjoyment is very dear to Krishna.

Ambition here is of two meanings, one to excel in work without expecting any fruits from it and one to just enjoy material enjoyments.

If you have the ambition to excel in your work as an offering to Krishna.

Than that is fine. But ambition for material is enjoyment is just a source of miseries.

One who is neither too happy in his achievement, nor too sad in his failure who neither laments, nor desires.who can renounce both the auspicious and inauspicious things Such a devotee is very dear to Krishna.

Too much of happiness is a sign for upcoming distress. One can escape duality of life by simply taking up to devotional Service.

So one who is equal in both happiness and distress, heal and cold, honor and dishonour, fame and infamy, always free from contaminating association, is silent and satisfied with everything, who is in full knowledge and is always engaged in the devotional service to Krishna is very dear to Krishna.

Krishna says at the last: "Those who follow this imperishable path of devotional service with complete faith making me as the supreme god of life,such a person is very, very dear to me.'

This devotional service, in the end will give unlimited divine pleasure away from material contamination.

Chapter Thirteen
Nature, the Enjoyer and Consciousness.

As we move through the chapters of Bhagavad Gita, Krishna with now tell us the practical implementations and knowledge of his teachings. In this chapter he will differentiate between the body, the soul and the super soul.

Arjuna asked, "O Krishna, I want to know more about nature, the enjoyer, the field and its knower, knowledge and its object".

The Supreme Personality of the Godhead said: "This body is called the field and one who knows this body is the knower of the field."

One should know that even Krishna is the knower of bodies. And to understand the body and its knower is called knowledge. That is Krishna's opinion.

Now Krishna will tell about this field of activity and how it is constituted, what are its changes, when it is Produced, who its Knower is and what his influences are.

The knowledge of the field and its knower is described by various sages in various Vedic scriptures. It is especially mentioned in Vedanta-sutra reasoning as to cause and effect.

The knowledge shared by Krishna is the Bhagavad Gita which is the essence of all the knowledge of the vedas.

The field of activities is considered to be the five great elements, false ego, intelligence, the unmanifested, the ten senses and the mind, five sense objects [form, smell, sound, taste, and touch], desire, hatred, happiness, distress, the aggregate and the life symptoms. So basically, our material body is made up of all the elements.

Humility, pridelessness, nonviolence, tolerance, simplicity, going to a bonafide spiritual master, cleanliness, steadiness, self-control, giving up the objects of sense gratification, absence of false ego, having the knowledge of the evil cycle of birth, death, old age and disease, detachment, freedom from the entanglement of material world even mindedness, unalloyed devotional service to Krishna, having the aspiration to live in a secluded place, detachment from a crowd, understand and accept the importance of self-realization, and search for the absolute truth. All these is declared knowledge by Krishna and rest all is ignorance.

The real definition of knowledge is what gives bliss to your soul and what frees or liberates you from the endless cycle of birth and death.

Krishna is one by one opening all the confidential secrets of life. He will now explain the knowledge, after knowing which you will taste the eternal.

He said; "Brahman, the spirit, beginning less and subordinate to me, which lies beyond the cause and effect of this material world". Which means that it does not have a reason nor the result. All the things in this world have a reason which have a reason which ends up in resulting something.

Krishna is talking about the super soul. We have a body, and beyond this body is our soul. And in this soul lies the super soul which is a potency of Krishna himself.

He further says that the Super soul exists which is with his hands and legs everywhere, his ears, heals and faces are all pervading.

The Supersoul is the source of all the senses yet he is away from the senses. Although, he is the maintainer of every living entity, he is unattached and is self- satisfied. He is the master of the three modes of material nature, but at same time he is aloof from them.

The Supreme person or the super soul exists both outside and inside of every living entity, even the moving and non moving. He is beyond our mundane material senses to see or know. He is far away from all of us yet, he is very near to each and everyone.

This means that although Krishna eternally resides in the spiritual divine abode. He is there situated as the Supersoul in our heart.

The supersoul is undivided, yet he divides himself among the living entities.

He is the maintainer off all but deveours and develops all.

The Supersoul is the source of light in all luminous objects. Beyond the darkness of matter, he is also unmanifested. He is the real knowledge, the object of knowledge, and the goal of our knowledge.

Krishna here told all the qualities of him [the Supersoul] which is his divine potency residing in our hearts.

So, the field of activities [the body], the knowledge and the knowable in a summarized version. But he says that only his devotees can understand this thoroughly and properly and will attain his nature.

Krishna further said. "the material world is made up of material nature [prakriti] and living entities[parasa]. They are considered to be beginingless. Their transformation and matter are all products of material nature."

Krishna is now telling about the material nature and the living entities coming from it.

He further says that this material nature is said to be the cause of material causes and effect, while the living entity is the cause of various sufferings and enjoyments in this material world.

Whatever we do, we do it under the influence of the three modes of material nature [goodness, passion and ignorance] and enjoy the good and bad fruits of it.

This cycle continues until and unless one engages oneself in the loving devotional service of Krishna.

He thus continues to follow the ways of life and enjoy the three modes of material nature. Due to his association with them, he will attain good or evil species in his next life.

Those who do actions under the influence of goodness, they attain form among demigods. Those who do it under the mode of passion, they attain human form and those who do it under the mode of ignorance attain animal form.

The field of activities (body) acts according to the values provided to it and according to its association with the three modes of material.

But yet in this body, within our hearts is another supreme and transcendental enjoyer who is the overseer and the sanctioner and is also the Supersoul.

Krishna further says : "Those who understand this philosophy of material nature [prakriti] and the interaction between the living entity [purusa] with the three modes of material nature is sure to be delivered from ocean of births and deaths. Regardless of his position in the present."

Krishna says to thoroughly understand the knowledge of prakriti und purusa and various interactions between them and such a person is also said to be liberated.

He further explains that some understand the Supersoul through meditation, other by the cultivation of knowledge [body, soul and supersoul] and still other by working without frutive desires of they do not except any fruits from their actions and simply fulfill their duty.

There are some people again who are not elevated spiritually so much but much but still develop a desire to worship the Supreme Lord, Krishna by hearing about him from the association of devotees. And such a person is also liberated.

So Krishna Says;" O Arjuna, know that whatever you see in this creation existing [moving or non moving] is just a combination of the field of activities and the knower of the field.

One who always sees the supersoul with soul and understands that they are indestructible with this destructible body is the one who actually sees.

One who sees the supersoul equally present everywhere in all living entities reaches the transcendental position.

He who knows and can see that all his activities are performed by for the body which is created by the material nature and he alone [as a soul] does not do anything actually sees.

One who is in knowledge can understand this difference between the body and the Soul and the supersoul and sees the truth. Rest all is false conception of life wherein most living entities live like animals, without knowledge and die wasting their life. And thus attains the next body and this cycle for him continues.

Where as a sensible man sees this difference and understands that every action that he does is due to his association with the three modes of material nature (goodness, passion and ignorance) and sees how beings are expanded everywhere.

Those who have the vision that everything in this material world has a cause but a soul is without cause and is transcendental, eternal and indestructible beyond the three modes of material nature. He, although being in contact with the body never does anything or entangles

The Sky due to its subtle nature, is all pervading but cannot be mixed with anything. Similarly, the soul does mix with the body all though it is situated in the body.

As then Sun illuminates the entire universe with its light, the body is illuminated by the soul with its consciousness. Therefore, making the body move.

As a conclusion for this chapter, Krishna Says "One who sees the difference between the body and its knower with eyes of knowledge. And can also understand the process of liberation from the bondage of the material world attain to the Supreme goal".

Chapter Fourteen
The Three Modes of Material Nature

We have heard that the material Nature is made up of the three modes namely goodness, passion & ignorance and everything and everyone acts according to these three modes of nature. In this chapter, Krishna will talk about them and how can one conquer or go beyond these three modes.

The Supreme Personality of Godhead said: "O Arjuna, Once again, I repeat the best of all knowledge after knowing which great sages have attained the Supreme Position."

By becoming fixed in this knowledge, one becomes situated in the transcendental nature of Supreme. And is not born at the time of creation nor disturbed at the time of annihilation or destruction, of this cosmic manifestation.

Krishna is repeating again and again that by becoming situated in the divine, one can be freed from the cycle of birth and death.

In this material world, the Brahman is the source of all births taking place for all the species of life. And that Brahman comes from Krishna.

Krishna further says:" All Species of life come into existence or are made possible by taking place in the material world. And I am the seed-giving father.

Krishna is-source of all possible lives in the material world.

This material nature is made up of three modes - goodness, passion & ignorance. They act upon everything in this material world and when a living entity comes In contact with them he becomes conditioned by them. All these three modes binds a living entity to the fruits of his actions.

The mode others of goodness is purer than all other modes. A living entity in contact with the mode of goodness always engages himself in doing pious activities and finding knowledge. But this mode conditions a person to material happiness and knowledge. And such a person cannot think of Krishna who is beyond these three mode.

The mode of passion binds a living entity from the fruits of his actions. A living entity has endless desires within him.

The mode of ignorance is born from darkness. A living entity in contact with this mode is always in a state of madness doing impious works. It also includes tee State of -intoxication, and also results in laziness such as day-dreaming.

In summary, the mode of goodness conditions one to happiness, A man is extreme material happiness cannot perform devotional Service to Krishna and it binds him. The mode of passion conditions one to frutive actions and the mode of ignorance conditions one to madness.

Krishna further explains that there is always a competition between these three modes of material nature. Sometimes goodness defeats passion & ignorance, sometimes passion defeats goodness & ignorance and sometimes ignorance defeats goodness & passion.

When all the nine gates of the body are filled with divine knowledge, the increase in the mode of goodness is felt.

When we have unlimited desires, fruitive actions, attachment within his, there is an increase in the mode of passion.

For example, when a man earns Some amount of money, his greed for earning more increases. So, basically after he gets the money that satisfies his & his family's needs, he still does not stop and has the greed for earning more. This shows that there is an increase in the mode of passion.

Most with of us are simply dwelling the mode of passion just think to enjoy the fruits of our actions, as which are happiness, distress and disrespect and honour, etc.

With the increase in the mode of ignorance, one's life revolves around darkness, madness, illusion, etc.

When a person dies with the mode of goodness, he attains the heavenly planets of great sages in the higher planetary system.

When a person dies in the mode of passion, he takes birth among men doing fruitive actions. When a person dies in the mode of ignorance he attains animal life.

This is a fair justice done by Krishna. Depending on the tree you plant, you will accordingly get the fruit.

The actions done in the mode of goodness, its results are pure. Those actions which are done in the mode of passion result in on misery or distress. Though, we don't know it but most of the time we are associating with the mode of passion and end up getting troubles and miseries. The actions done in the mode of ignorance result in madness.

Real-knowledge develops from the mode of goodness. From the mode of passion, greed develops. And the from the mode of ignorance, develops illusion.

Those who are situated in the mode of goodness go to the higher heavenly planets. Those situated in the mode of passion remain on the earthly planets and those who are associating with the mode of ignorance go to the lower hellish planets.

Krishna further says: "Those who can see that there is no other doer than these three modes of material nature and knows the Supreme Lord is beyond and transcendental to all these three modes attain to my spiritual nature."

These three modes control a person completely. And the person doesn't know that he is forced to work according to them.

When a living entity is able to escape these three modes escape of material nature. He will be freed from birth, death old age and various types of distress. And he can enjoy the real bliss of life.

All these modes bind us and ultimately we end go up getting troubles. So the one who is satisfied and knows that all the pleasures of this world are temporary and does not run behind theme but instead works for Krishna and for the pleasure of Krishna attains peace and happiness.

Arjuna asked: "O Lord, what are the symptoms shown by the person who is beyond these three modes of material nature? And how can one transcend the modes of materials nature as every action we do, it is under the influence of these modes?

The Supreme Personality of Godhead answered: "One who does not hate these three modes [illumination, attachment. and delusion] whether they are present or not. Who is not disturbed through all the reactions of his material actions."

"One who remains neutral and transcendental as he knows that the modes are the actual doer. One who is self-situated and remains same in happiness, distress."

"One who looks upon a Stone and a piece of gold with equal eye, which means of gold that he does not have greed for them as all are equal for him."

"One who is equal towards everyone, situated equally in honour, and dishonour. Who treats both friends and enemy equally and who has renounced all the material activities, such a person is said to have transcended these three modes."

Krishna further says that one who is constantly engaged in his devotional Service is able to transcend all these three modes of material abure and Position of Brahman.

So we should do all the work as a service to Krishna.

Krishna is the basis of impersonal Brahman, who is immortal and imperishable. He is the supreme constitutional position for ultimate happiness.

In the conclusion has exposed we can say that Krishna has exposed all the three modes Material nature to us. And our goal is to transcend them and attain to the spiritual nature of Krishna.

Chapter Fifteen
The Yoga of the Supreme Person

Who are we? Why are we living? What is the purpose of our life? What is the goal of life? These Questions must have occurred inside your mind. If not than you need to check your association, Krishna tells that we are souls and our ultimate purpose is to detach from the material world and understand Krishna. Well, that is what this chapter is about.

The Supreme Personality of Godhead "said it is said that there is and imperishable banyan tree of this material world whose roots are upwards and branches are downwards. The Leaves of this trees have Vedic hyms written on it and its knower is said should to be the Knower of the Vedas."

The Branches of this tree extend both upwards and downwards. The roots of this tree are always strong and growing are as they are nourished by three modes material nature. These roots are bound to frutive activities. The tree has all the 84 lakh species of life. The fruits growing on this tree are of happiness and distress and we living entities as birds on a tree are always eating these fruits of our actions.

The real form of this tree is not understandable while we are in this material world. As this tree is unlimited because we don't know where it ends or from where it is starting.

However, the person who has cut down the roots of this tree by the weapon of detachment can see the form of this tree.

After doing this, he must surrender unto the Supreme Personality of Godhead, Krishna whom everything started and in whom everything will dissolve.

We always want to have a false Status in the material Society. But Krishna says that those who are free from this false prestige, illusion and association. Those who understand the eternal. Who are free from lust. We know that it is fixed that- after happiness, distress will come, after victory, defeat will come. It is fixed like seasons. Those who escape this duality of life, know how to Surrender and attain to the Supreme eternal kingdom.

Krishna further said, "The Supreme abode of mine is not illuminated by sun or moon, or fire or electricity. But those who reach it, never return to this Material world.

The Sun illuminates this entire world and universe. But Krishna's supreme abode, which is the Goloka Vrindavan Dham is so effulgent that it does not require any material source of light to illuminate itself. And the living entity which goes there will never return against to the house of miseries.

The living entities born in this conditioned world are eternally parts of Krishna. But due to the qualities obtained by the three Modes of material nature, they keep Struggling with the six senses which include the mind.

When a person dies, his body remains in this world but his soul is carried to another body with his previous life's conceptions.

When he gets another gross body the cycle of getting a set of senses which includes a type of ear, eye, nose, and, sense of touch according to the type of body will continue.

But conceptions of life means that whatever qualities a person's mind has obtained in the previous life. He will continue to do the karma according to those qualities irrespective of the type of body.

For example, if one has done impious activities in the previous life his mind will attain those qualities and he will continue to do those type of Karma. When on the other hand if one has progressed on the path of devotional service he will continue in this next birth.

The foolish men cannot understand how one attains body and enjoys a set up Senses under the three modes of material nature. But one whose eye are well trained in knowledge can see all this.

The transcendentalists who are well trained in knowledge and are situated in self-realization can clearly see all these changes, Whereas the people who are not situated in self- realization cannot see them, though they may try to.

When the light of the sun falls on the world it removes all the darkness. Krishna says, that this splendor of the sun, the moon and the fire are from him.

The Scientists say that the sun gives out light-due to fusion in itself. But the cause of that fusion is Krishna as he himself says that he is the primeval cause of all causes.

Krishna enters into each planet and by his energy, all the planets stay in their orbit. He is the supplier of the juice of Life in the vegetables which we eat.

We eat food to stay alive in this material body. These are four types of food:

- Which can be chewed
- Which can be dranked
- Which can be licked
- Which can be Sucked

Krishna says that he is fire which causes digestion in our body, and the air and air of life, which comes out goes in to digest all these four kinds of foodstuff

Krishna further says: "I am there seated in everyone's heart, from me comes remembrance, knowledge and forgetfulness. From the Vedas, I am only to be known and I am the compiler of the Vedanta. Whatever good or bad happens in a Person's life it is due to Krishna".

Krishna says these again and again so that we understand that he is the Supreme Lord.

All living beings are divided into two Classes: the falliable and the infeliable. All the living entities in this material world are falliable or destructible as the body dies. But those in the spiritual world are infalliable or indestructible.

But apart from these two classes there is one greatest living personality which is the Supreme Personality of Godhead, Krishna himself. The one who enters into all the three worlds and maintains them.

As Krishna is transcendental and beyond these two classes of beings and that is why he is praised and worshiped in the both the world and the Vedas as the Supreme person.

One who knows that Krishna is the Supreme Personality of Godhead is without a doubt, the knower of everything and he will engage in the devotional service of Krishna without arrogance or ego.

Krishna further says, "This was the most confidential part of the Vedas which is now disclosed by me. And whoever will understand this will endeavor for perfection. "

In conclusion to this chapter, Krishna has exposed all the summary of the Vedas here. So one should take full advantage of this and engage in the loving Service of Krishna.

Chapter Sixteen
The Divine and Demonic Natures

We learnt that there are two classes of living beings. But the human nature is divided again into two departments - Divine & Demonic. Different people react differently in same situations. But why is it so? This question is answered by Krishna in this chapter. And what are the symptoms of such people and why are they put into these categories of divine & demonic.

The Supreme Personality of Godhead said: "One who is free from fear, who is purified of his existence, who has spiritual knowledge, who does charity [Espiritually more], who performs various sacrifices. the [Hare Krishna maha mantra is only sacrifice for kalyuga]"

"Who studies various Vedic scriptures, who performs austerity, who is simple in nature, who supports non-violence [it here means that you should spread more & more Krishna consciousness. One who does not to do Set is also considered an act of violence], who always speaker truth."

"Who is free from anger also has renunciation for detachment, tranquility, who does not find fault in others, who is gentle, modest, and has steady determination, vigor and the ability to forgive, fortitude. Who Keeps hygiene both external and internal."

"Who is not jealous of others, who is not happy after being honored by others [as it satisfies his false ego] These are the transcendental qualities of people with divine nature."

Now, Krishna will tell about people with demonic natures. They are simply the opposite of people with divine natures.

He says, "One with pride, arrogance, anger, who is harsh towards others, and has ignorance are those with demonic natures."

The transcendental or divine qualities lead to liberation from this world but the demonic qualities Cause more and more bondage to this material world. As Arjuna was born with divine qualities, Krishna is giving this Knowledge to him.

So clearly, Krishna has classified all the living beings into divine all & demonic. He has already told in detail about the people with divine natures, now he will tell about people with demonic nature.

He says: "Those are of demonic natures don't know is right and what is wrong or what to do and what not to do. They neither keep hygiene nor are they polite towards others nor truth is found in them. Neither are they pure internally as well as externally."

"As the people with divine qualities do activities that are constructive for the world. These people with demonic natures are always lost in their lust and do actions that are meant to destroy this world."

"They take Shelter of the lust which insatiable and are always in conceit of their false pride. They do unclean and impious work and are always attracted to the temporary."

One should always try to stay away from the association of these people with demonic natures.

One primary symptom that is found in these people of demonic nature is that they always want sense gratification and believe that it is the main purpose of life Due to this the anxiety in them is immeasurable.

To enjoy sense gratification these People can do any illegal work.

These people are always in ignorance and think, "I have so much wealth now, I will gain more tomorrow. This is all mine now which will keep increasing further."

"He is my enemy, I have killed him and I will kill all of them. I am the lord, I am the enjoyer of everything. I am perfect, the most powerful and the richest."

So basically these people indirectly think themselves as god as they believe that they are only the enjoyer. But the people with divine natures always perform Sacrifices for the pleasure of the supreme lord, Krishna and do not think themselves as the enjoyer of everything.

Thus, the people with demonic natures are bound by illusions and suffer from various anxieties and go down to hell.

These people always illusioned by wealth and false prestige perform sacrifices without any rules and regulations but- just to maintain their false position in the society.

The people of demonic natures are always lost in lust and think that they are only the supreme enjoyer and no other is greater or equal to them. So they are always jealous of Krishna who is the Supreme Personality of godhead. The fact being that Krishna is present as supersoul in their bodies but still they do not serve him.

These people are considered lower among men-and Krishna puts them again and again into material existence and in the demonic species of life.

It is not like Krishna does partiality to these people or does not love them. He clearly says that he is equal to everyone and even these people get a choice whether they want to perform devotional service or not.

But still if they pick up to do impious works, Krishna will accordingly set the consequences.

Krishna further says:" when they attain repeated births in demonic species of life, they fall down to the lowest type and can never come to me."

In this age of Kalyuga, we can see a majority of people are the one with demonic natures.

Krishna further says that there are three doors to hell - lust, anger and greed.

Now, this is a very important point. The people who have lust, anger and greed in them are always struggling and are always in distress. Krishna causes the degradation of Soul or one may fall to lower levels. Krishna recommends us to give up these emotions.

Even Krishna says that it is lust only which causes one to do sinful actions.

One who has conquered lust, anger and greed always perform actions of Self- realization. And they reach the Supreme destinations.

On the other hand, one who does karma according to his own will without the rules given in the Vedic scriptures neither gets perfection, happiness nor the supreme destination.

Therefore, in order to get elevated to higher levels, one who should perform duty by knowing it properly from the Vedic scriptures. The most important of them being the Bhagavad Gita, which is spoken by the Supreme Personality of Godhead, Krishna himself.

In conclusion to this chapter, Krishna says that although some people are of demonic natures, but we should not hate them as we must have compassion for every living entity. But we should stay away from the association of such people. To make ourselves more & more divine so that we can serve the Supreme Personality of Godhead, Krishna and people would love us.

Chapter Seventeen
The divisions of Faith

As we learnt about the three modes of material nature. There are three types of faith associated with theme Faith associated with the mode of passion & ignorance Cause bondage to this material nature. Whereas faith associated with the mode of goodness, help us cross the three modes and enter into divinity. Although even the mode of goodness binds us to knowledge and satisfactions and we may not perform devotional service to Krishna.

Arjuna Said:" Krishna, the people who perform Sacrifices or actions according to their own will and imagination without following the principles given in Vedic scriptures, Are they in goodness, passion or ignorance?"

The Supreme Personality of Godhead answered: "A soul acquires one of the three modes of material nature in majority. And of- according to it his faith is established three types - in goodness, passion or ignorance.

So basically our soul is under the influence of the three modes of material nature as long as we don't perform devotional Service to Krishna. By associating with them we develop a faith in these three modes.

One who is in goodness worships the demigods. One who is in passion worships the demons sand one who is in ignorance worships the ghost or spirit.

So according to our faith, so is the object of worship.

If one thinks that by associating with mode of goodness, one can be liberated then it is not like that. Though, it is considered as superior to the other two modes. Even the mode of goodness binds us to the material world. But it can help you to get into divinity.

Krishna further says that those who perform various sacrifices, penances, etc but with the attitude of pride and ego whose mind is in lust and attachment. Those who torture with material elements of the body and even the Supersoul [Krishna] who is there in every living entity's heart are said to be as demons.

These three modes of material nature even affect the food we eat, sacrifices, penances, and charity.

Those who have their faith associated in the mode of goodness. Eat the food which purifies oneself. Which gives pleasure to one's heart, give strength & happiness this food is characterized as juicy, fatty, wholesome.

Those who are associated be with the mode of passion eat food which too salty, too bitter, too hot & spicy: This food is the food of extremes. This gives distress, misery and causes diseases in oneself.

Those associated with the mode of ignorance eat food which was prepared more than three hours before eating, which does not have any taste, and is of bad Smell consisting of things which are untouchable. Meat and eggs also come this category,

However, a food which is beyond all there three modes is the Prasadam offered to Krishna which has so much Potency that it can take us to the Supreme abode of Krishna.

When it comes to sacrifices, when one performs sacrifices as they are prescribed in the Vedic Scriptures, just to please the Supreme Lord, Krishna without wanting any personal benefit is a sacrifice performed in the mode of goodness.

For example if one chants the Hare Krishna mantra [sacrifice for kalyuga] just to please or for the satisfaction of Krishna, it is a sacrifice performed in the mode of goodness.

However, if one performs Sacrifices for his own personal benefit, is a sacrifice performed in mode of passion.

For example the chanting of the Hare Krishna mantra just get some material pleasure or benefit from Krishna. It is Just like doing business with Krishna.

But if one performs sacrifices without following the principle of the Vedic Scriptures and by his own imagination without giving charity, offering prasadam, improper chanting, is a sacrifice performed in the mode of ignorance.

When it comes to Austerity, the austerities of the body include the worshiping Supreme Lord, Krishna, the Brahmanas, your spiritual master (god), your superiors who are your parents. This worship should be done in hygiene, simplicity and in non-violence.

Austerities of speech include in chanting Vedic hyms [Hare Krishna mantra for Kalyuga], speaking words which are truthful, sweet and pleasing to others your words should not hurt someone.

Austerities of mind include that the mind should be simple, self-controlled and satisfied. This purifies one's existence. Krishna further says that when these three types of austerities which are of body, speech and mind. are performed to please lord Krishna without expecting anything for our own benefit is said to be austerity in the mode of goodness.

However, when the same austerities are performed just for the sake of our own benefit, it is said to be performed in the mode of passion.

When these austerities are performed with a foolish mind and with the intent of causing harm to others are said to be performed in the mode of ignorance.

When it comes to charity, the charity which is given as a matter of duty, without expecting anything in return, at a correct place & time and to the person who deserves it is said to be performed in the mode of goodness.

But when this charity is given to attain some material benefit or in a mood of grudge is said to be performed in the mode of passion. This type of charity is most common in kalyuga. When charity is given at a place which is not proper, time is also not proper and to the person who does not deserve, and without respect is said to be performed in the mode of ignorance.

Krishna further said: "From the start of the entire creation, the three spiritual words Om, tat and Sat indicates the Supreme Personality of Godhead. These words were used by the Brahmanas and holy spirits while chanting Vedic hyms to please the supreme Lord."

Hence, transcendental people take shelter of these words and perform charity, penances, and austerities without expecting anything always attain the supreme.

By uttering the word 'tat' and performing various sacrifices without expecting any reward, one can be freed from material bondage.

The Supreme Personality of Godhead, Krishna is the absolute on only truth.

And truth is indicated by the word Sat. All kinds of sacrifices are performed to please the Supreme truth come under the word Sat or truth.

But any sacrifice, be it charity, penance, etc performed without having faith in the Supreme Lord is not a truth and is called asat, which is completely the opposite of sat. It is useless in every life.

Thus, in conclusion to this chapter, we can say that Material world by everything in this are the games played the three modes of material nature. By understanding and escaping them one can enter into divine knowledge and Serve Krishna.

Chapter Eighteen
Conclusion – The Perfection of Renunciation

As we flip through more & more Pages of Bhagavad Gita, we have now reached the last and the final Chapter. In this chapter, Krishna will give the ultimate message of Bhagavad Gita to all of us. Which is, that the ultimate goal of life is to surrender to the Supreme Personality of Godhead (Krishna) which will free us from all kinds of sins and we go home, back to godhead. This chapter is also a revision of the previous seventeen chapters..

Arjuna said: "O Supreme Lord, I want to know more about renunciation (tyāga) and of the renounced order of life (Sanyasa)."

"Tyaga and 'Sanyasa" look the same but there is a difference between the two teams, which Arjuna is asking...

The Supreme Personality of Godhead said: When one gives up all the activities which are based on material desire which means that he does not do anything for his own benefit is what learned men call renounced order of life (Sanyasa) . And giving up the fruits or the result of all the activities is said to be the renunciation. (tyaga)

So basically, there is a very subtle difference between both the teams which we need to pay attention at.

Usually people think that giving up the life of a householder is sanyasa but actually giving up the activities which we do for our own benefit and instead doing it for the benefit of Krishna is what is Sanyasa.

Krishna further says that some learned men think that all frutive activities are faulty or wrong and hence should be given up. However, great sages continue to do the acts of sacrifice, Charity and penance and think that they should be never abandoned.

However, Krishna further declares his judgment over renunciation (tyaga) which are or three kinds.

Krishna says that acts of sacrifice, charity and penance should be done as they purify one's soul.

All of these actions or activities must be performed but without the attachment- of its fruit or result and only as a matter of duty.

So, when it comes to tyaga, Krishna Says to leave the result of the work, not the work.

All those activities which are for the benefit of Krishna and which are recommended by the Vedic scriptures are considered to be prescribed duties.

Krishna says that these prescribed duties must never be renounced. If one renounces these duties the renunciation is said to be in the mode of ignorance.

Anyone who feels that his prescribed duties are causing trouble to him or thinks that they will cause him bodily discomfort. For example struggling at the beginning of one's career, earning money, and leaves his duties, then such a renunciation is said to be in the mode of Passion. Such a person cannot be elevated to higher levels of renunciation.

But the person who performs his duties only because it is ought to be done and for the Pleasure of Krishna and renounces the fruits on results of it, then it is said to be in the mode of goodness.

This type of renouncer is said to be in the mode of goodness and he neither hates the inauspicious work nor is attached to the auspicious work and perfectly understands work according to Krishna.

The unlimited cycle of births & deaths continues until and unless one realizes the presence of supersoul or Krishna within him and surrenders unto him.

As Krishna says that values of your previous life are transferred previous to your next life, it is almost impossible for any living entity to give up all activities. And the one who renounces the results of his activities said to be truly renounced.

One who is not renounced and is engaged in furtive activities there are three Kinds of fruits to his actions:

* Desirable
* Undesirable
* Mixed.

These people have to suffer or enjoy these fruits. But, one who is renounced will not have to suffer or enjoy.

Krishna further explains to Arjuna that there are five factors responsible for the accomplishment of an action. These are:

* The place where the action happened! (Body)
* The one who performs the action. (The soul)
* The different types of actions (Karma)
* The different kinds of endeavors (Desires)
* The Supersoul (Krishna).

Whatever action a man performs; may it be right or wrong, performed by the body or mind or speech is caused by all these five factors.

One who thinks that he is the only doer and does not consider all these five factors told by Krishna is not intelligent according Krishna. He is not able to see things as they are.

Such a person should take into account that no work or action can be accomplished without the sanction of the Supreme Personality of Godhead (Krishna).

Krishna recommends that the person who does work only for the pleasure of Krishna and is not motivated by false ego and his intelligence is not entangled, He kills men, but still does not kill. He will be bound by his actions. This does not mean that we can do wrong works which aren't it reccomended in the Vedic Scriptures.

For example, 'Arjuna thought that he is the doer and did not notice the Sanction of Krishna or the supreme Lord. Therefore when Krishna enlightened him with the knowledge of Bhagavad Gita He fought, but for the pleasure of Krishna.

Because Krishna wanted him to fight. And thus, was not bounded by his action.

In this way, one should perform all his duties, but only for the pleasure of Krishna, to make Krishna happy. And not for his known personal benefit .

Krishna further says: 'The Three Factors that motivate action are knowledge, the object of knowledge. And the knower of the knowledge. Furthermore, the senses, the work and the doer are the three constituents of actions.'

The knowledge, the action happening and its performer and can be categorized according to the three modes of material nature (goodness, passion & ignorance).

When it comes to a knowledge, when a person sees everything one, under a single spiritual nature divided among many living enties, it is considered to be in the mode of goodness. Such a person sees all persons to be equal. He considers them as a soul, which is a part and Parcel of the Supreme personality of Godhead.

The knowledge which forces one to see a different type of living entity in every body, For example: we consider some person to be rich, the other to be poor, others to be white, while the others to be black. Such a Knowledge is considered to be in the mode of passion.

The knowledge which forces one to be attached to only one kind of work, without thinking about right or wrong. And which is too small in amount is considered to be in the mode of ignorance.

When it comes to action, the action which prescribed in the scriptures, which is performed with the intention to serve the supreme Personality of Godhead, without any attachment and expectation of fruits mode is considered to be in the mode of goodness.

But when the same action is performed with the intention to fulfill one's material desires and with a sense of false ego it is considered to be in the mode of passion.

The action recommended performed, which is not in the Vedic scriptures, without thinking that it will cause great material bondage in future and with the intention of causing harm on distress to others is considered to be in the mode of ignorance.

When it comes to the performer of the action, one who performs the action as a matter of duty. Without associating with the three modes of material nature, without the sense of false ego, with lots of enthusiasm and determination, without thinking of failure or success or considered as a worker in the mode of goodness.

The worker who is attached to the work and performs it to enjoy the fruits (sense gratification). Who is always gereedy, jeaslous or envious of others, impure and is entangled between the dualities of life (joy and sorrow, Victory and defeat, etc...) is considered to be in the mode of passion.

The worker who is always engaged in actions that are restricted in the Vedic Scriptures, performs actions which are materialistic, refuses to do the right action, cheating and who always insults others. One who is angry or morose and delays work (procrastination) is considered to be in the mode of ignorance.

So now, Krishna has told about the different types of knowledge, action and performer according to the three modes of material nature. But in our consciousness lies understanding as well as determination.

Krishna further says: "O Arjuna! now please hear the different types of understanding and determination according to the three modes of material nature."

When it comes to understanding, understanding by which one the knows what is to be done and what is not to be done, what is to be feared and what is to not be feared, which work can cause bondage and which words can Cause liberation is considered to be in the mode of goodness.

The understanding by which one cannot differentiate between what is right and what is wrong. What is a person supposed to do and what not, is considered to be in the mode of passion.

On the other hand, the understanding which thinks everything opposite, it considers the religion to be irreligion and irreligion to be religion is considered to be in mode of ignorance. It always forces one to the right wrong thing.

When it comes to determination, the determination, which cannot be breaked, derived by the yoga practice. And which can Control the activities of the mind, life and senses is considered in the mode of goodness.

The determination by which binds one to results of actions in religion, economic development and sense gratification is considered to be in the mode of passion.

The determination derived from illusion and which always, thinks about dreaming, fear, anger, and cannot go beyond them is considered to be in the mode of ignorance.

The Supreme Personality of Godhead Said: "O Arjuna, now hear from me, the three kinds of happiness derived from the three modes of material nature By which a conditioned living entity enjoys and sometimes comes to the end of distress."

So now, when it comes to happiness, the happiness which feels like poison or not very good at the Starting but at the end feels very good like nectar is considered to be in the mode of goodness. For example, devotional service to the lord may feel very boring at the beginning but feels like nectar at the end.

The happiness which feels very good like nectar at starting but ends winter poison is considered to be in the mode of passion. For example Sense gratification may feel like it is very good. But at end it feels like poison.

The happiness, which sees self-realization as nothing and is derived from illusion or delusion end. Which comes from beginning to from laziness and sleep is considered to be in the mode of ignorance.

So, now Krishna has told about the types of knowledge, action, and worker or performer, understanding, determination and happiness according to the three modes of materiel nature. However, beyond there these three modes, there is another mode or quality which is divine or transcendental which only comes and performing by serving Krishna unalloyed devotional service at his lotus feet.

Krishna further says" There is no living entity existing neither in there would nor in the heaven or other higher planetary system who is free from the three modes of material nature.

Now Krishna will tell us about the caste system:

* Brahmanas
* kshatriyas
* Vaishyas
* Shuduas.

We think that the caste System is categorized on the basis of our birth.

However according to Krishna every living entity associates with the three modes of material nature and on bases of the activities he does, he is categorized according to the caste system.

The qualities of Brahmana' are: He is always at peace, he is Self-Controlled, he is pure, tolerant and honest. In addition, austerity, knowledge wisdom and religiousness are more qualities that a Brahman has.

The qualities of a Kshatriya are: Heroism, resourcefulness, he is powerful and determines and Shouts courage, generosity and leadership in battle or war.

The qualities of a Vaishya are: Business, farming, protecting cows.

A Shudra is short of knowledge and therefore his only business are labour and service to others.

A living entity associates with the three modes of material nature and obtains these qualities based on which he is categorized in the caste system. It does not depend upon the birth, even if a person born in Shudra family exhibits a Brahman's qualities he is called as a Brahmana in the caste system and vice versa..

Krishna further says:" Any man can become perfect when follows the qualities of his work. Now hear from me, how?"

Actually this caste system is actually known as Varna System. Many people think that the shudra class is a lower class. But each and every class has its prescribed duty. Brahmans are the educators, Kshatriyas are the administrators, Vaishyas are the people can profit from business and Shudras are the service executors who can earn from Salary.

So each and every class in the Varna system is equally important for the human society.

Krishna further says that a person of any class should perform his prescribed duty as a worship of the Supreme Lord, and by doing so, he attains perfection.

According to Krishna, it is better to perform one's own prescribed duty imperfectly than to interfere in someone's duty and perform it perfectly. As by doing one's own duty, he is never affected by sinful reactions.

One should never give up his duty although there might be some fault in it.

Like this, Krishna encourages everyone to perform their duties without expectation of fruits and offering them to him.

By performing one's duties, he may achieve the supreme perfection. This is done by being self-controlled and unattached to material fruits or results and sense enjoyment, and by practicing renunciation.

Krishna further says;" O Arjuna, now please hear from me how one who has achieved perfection by performing one's duty and practicing renunciation car achieve the stage of highest Knowledge by acting in some ways."

A person can reach the position of Self-realization by being purified, controlling the mind with full determination. By giving up all objects for material sense enjoyment, being freed for attachment- and hatred and other dualities of life (happiness and distress, victory and defeat, etc).

By living in alone secluded place, controlling oneself and eating only per need. (Neither too much nor too less). One who is always situated in trance (highest position of Yoga), by practicing detachment.

By being freed from fake ego, strength, pride, lust, anger and free from the acceptance of materialistic pleasures. And being peaceful.

Such a person who is transcendentally situated, realizes the supreme absolute becomes joyful. He has no desire felt and performs pure devotional service to Krishna who is the supreme Personality of Godhead.

Krishna further says that only his devotee can understand him by performing devotional service to him.

Krishna again and again says to perform devotional service to his lotus feet is the only goal of life. And only such a person can enter the eternal abode of Krishna.

A devotee of Krishna does all the work and activities for the pleasure of Krishna, he completely depends upon Krishna for everything. He always thinks of Krishna in everything. And by the grace and protection of Krishna he enters the supreme eternal abode of Krishna.

If one always thinks of Krishna and does devotional service to him, he can cross any obstacle of life. But if one does not work for Krishna's pleasure and works under false ego will be lost according to Krishna's opinion, Krishna Says to Arjuna: "If you do not work under my direction and on do not carry out your duty of figuring, you will still have to fight as you are Kshatriya."

Krishna is trying to explain that one may decline to work under his direction but he will still have to do the Same nature because of his nature.

The difference is that if we do some activity for Krishna, it will liberate us, but if we do the same activity under our false ego, it will Cause bondage to this material world.

All the living entities are seated on a machine of material energy. Krishna is situated as supersoul in everyone's heart and controls there activities. And he therefore suggests to give up all material desire and surrender unto him and thus you are sure to attain transcendental peace and Supreme eternal abode of Krishna.

Krishna told to Arjuna: "I have now explained the knowledge which was more confidential than others. Please think up on it whole-heartedly and then you are free to do whatever you want."

This is indirectly a message for all of us. Krishna has given us the knowledge. It is his duty to guide fallen souls like us. But it completely depends on us whether we want to follow it or not. This shows that Krishna is very compassionate. Even after giving this supreme knowledge, he isn't forcing Arjuna to follow it.Like we are also given a chance to follow it or not.

Krishna further said: "Because you are my very intimate friend Arjuna, now I am giving my supreme instruction hear this for your benefit."

So now after giving all the knowledge Krishna is giving last and supreme instruction which will also be the Conclusion of Srimad Bhagavad Gita.

Krishna asks us to do four things

* Always think of him
* Become his devotee
* Worship him
* Offer obeisances unto him.

By doing these, one attain Krishna considers him to his very dear friend.

This same thing is repeated in Chapter Nine to lay importance on what Krishna actually wants us to do.

The most important thing said by Krishna in the Bhagavad Gita is: "Abandon all varieties of religion and simply surrender unto me. I shall liberate you from all sinful reactions. Do not fear"

We can see that in every chapter, Krishna had laid special emphasis on "devotional service." In the initial chapters he talks about Karma yoga, in chapter six, about the Astanga yoga, which is a meditational practice. But all these different types of yoga ultimately lead to Bhakti yoga "or devotional service. Which is the Supreme.

We can get devotional service by surrendering and being completely dependent on the all-pervasive Supreme Lord Krishna, and he assures you that he will liberate you from all sins of past lives. One should not fear and just work for the pleasure of the Supreme Personality of Godhead.

Krishna further says that this confidential knowledge cannot be explained to one who is not Pious, or devoted and does not perform devotional service to the Lord. Nor to the Person who is envious or jealous of Krishna.

One who does not believe in Krishna the knowledge of Bhagavad Gita would not benefit him.

Krishna guarantees pure devotional Service who will preach this knowledge to his devotees and he will surely come back to Krishna. And such a person or a devotee is the most dear to Krishna. Therefore, one should give or preaches knowledge to others and that is very dear to Krishna. When you give Krishna, you will get Krishna.

Krishna says: " I declare that whoever studies this conversation out of me and Arjuna will worship me with full devotion."

Thus, performing devotional Service is the concluding statement of Krishna.

In the Bhagavad Gita.

One who reads or hears this conversation between The Supreme Lord Krishna and Arjuna with full faith and devotion and without envy gets freed from all sinful reactions of past lives and attains pious auspicious planets.

Krishna asked, "O Arjuna, did you hear all my instructions with full attentions. Are your doubts and Illusion now cleared?"

Arjuna answered: "O My dear Krishna, The Supreme Lord I have now regained my memory, my illusion is now gone... I am free from al doubts and ready to act according to your instructions."

Sanjaya said, "Thus I have heard this beautiful conversation between Krishna and Arjuna, two great souls. My hair is standing on end after hearing this wonderful message."

"I am very lucky to have heard most confidential talks from the Supreme lord, Krishna the master of all mystic powers."

Even Sanjaya who was translating the whole battle of Mahabharata to Dhritrasthra was blessed to hear this Bhagavad Gita by the mercy of Krishna and Vyasa Deva.

Arjuna, who was very confused at the beginning of the battle was now relaxed and ready to work according to Krishna's instructions.

One who works for Krishna and according to Krishna will never have to face failure.

Sanjaya further said at: "O king, as I recall this conversation again and again, I feel pleasure. and I am thrilled at every moment.

"As I remember this very beautiful form of Lord Krishna, I am struck with wonder."

This shows that one who is engaged in the devotional service of Krishna he feels unlimited pleasure and joy which is beyond material happiness.

So, in conclusion to this chapter. We can say wherever there is Krishna, the Supreme Lord and Arjuna, the Supreme Archer and this conversation between the two, there will be opulence, power which is extraordinary and morality and certainly victory will be yours!!

Conclusion

Shrimad Bhagavad Gita is also called song of the God as it is a manual of life. Anyone who reads it sincerely with devotion towards Krishna is sure to never fall in his / her life as Krishna has promised that his devotee never falls or perishes.

Originally, we all are connected to Krishna. We as souls are eternally parts and parcels of Krishna. But, we have ended up being in this material world and are conditioned by the three modes of material nature. We have forgotten our eternal relationship with Krishna.

We are in a state of material consciousness currently. We think that the situations around us are the truth. But that isn't the case. The entire material creation is temporary and full of miseries.

We all are completed surrounded by dualities. Right now, there may be happiness, but the next moment miseries would come. Happiness and miseries, victory and defeat, respect and disrespect are all a part of this material creation working under maya or the three modes of material nature.

We spend our entire life engaging in this dualities. Now we may be happy and get loads of respect but at the next moment there may be hardships. Therefore Krishna instructs to tolerate all these dualities.

One who is neither too happy on achieving something or too sad on losing something is an ideal person.

We don't know how many lives we have spent working under this material nature. But, is it really our work to do?

Krishna concludes the Shrimad Bhagavad Gita by saying, "Abandon all types of religion and simply surrender unto me. I shall deliver you from all types of sinful reactions." Therefore this is the final instruction for all conditioned souls.

"TO ENGAGE IN THE DEVOTIONAL SERVICE OF KRISHNA."

That is the ultimate goal of this human form of life. Krishna urges each soul to not think of happiness or hardships, victory or defeat, gain or loss and simply work for the satisfaction of Krishna.

Practicing Krishna consciousness and preaching this divine message to everyone is the only duty of a soul. Rest all are just a part of life. One should not bother about his / her material conditions and simply work for Krishna and depend upon him. And Krishna ensures to take responsibility such a divine soul.

Just as all organs of our body work to satisfy the stomach, one should engage all his senses, mind, body and finally the soul in the loving service of Krishna. And finally go back home, back to Godhead. People generally think that I must practice devotional service in old age. However, there is no age or qualification required to practice Krishna consciousness. One may not be materially very qualified but if he is engaged in devotional service, he is to be considered divine.

Devotional service is very easy, Krishna says "Always think of me, become my devotee, worship me and offer your homage unto me" In in the age of Kali chanting of the divine Hare Krishna Maha Mantra is recommended as the topmost service to Krishna, without which one cannot become fully in love with Krishna.

One in a million souls get the opportunity to serve Krishna. The person who even endeavors or desires to serve Krishna is considered to be divine.

Therefore, keeping in mind that Krishna is the supreme personality of Godhead, the Supreme master and proprietor of everything engage in this Krishna consciousness, chant the Hare Krishna Maha Mantra, fall in love with him and rejoice into it.

www.ingramcontent.com/pod-product-compliance
Lightning Source LLC
LaVergne TN
LVHW061555070526
838199LV00077B/7059